The
125
MOST ASKED
QUESTIONS
About
DOGS

(and the answers)

Also by John Malone

The 125 Most Asked Questions About Cats

The
125
MOST ASKED
QUESTIONS
About
DOGS

(and the answers)

John Malone

WILLIAM MORROW AND COMPANY, INC.

New York

LIBRARY OF CONGRESS CATALOGING-IN-PUBLICATION DATA

Malone, John Williams.
The 125 most asked questions about dogs (and the answers) / by
John Malone.
p.   cm.
Includes bibliographical references and index.
ISBN 0-688-11311-7
1. Dogs—Miscellanea.   I. Title.   II. Title: One hundred twenty-
five most asked questions about dogs (and the answers).
SF426.M35   1993   92-38538
636.7—dc20   CIP

Printed in the United States of America

First Edition

1 2 3 4 5 6 7 8 9 10

BOOK DESIGN AND ILLUSTRATIONS BY KATHRYN PARISE

Contents

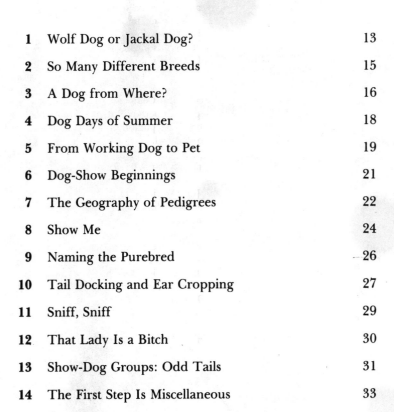

The
125
MOST ASKED
QUESTIONS
About
DOGS

(and the answers)

1

Wolf Dog or Jackal Dog?

Q: I had always assumed that dogs were descended from wolves, but I've recently heard a couple of people say that the real ancestor might be the jackal. *Is there any real evidence to suggest that the jackal might be the ancestor of the dog?*

A: The evidence for both the wolf and the jackal is pretty circumstantial. Wolves tend to run from humans, jackals hang around them; wolves howl, jackals bark—which so far seems to favor the jackal. But jackals exhibit an intense dislike for dogs. And wolf packs have a social structure that closely resembles that of wild dogs. Two points in favor of the wolf. Also, wolves were until recent times found almost everywhere on earth, and there were many different kinds of wolves in various parts of the world. These two facts help to explain the diversity of even the most ancient breeds of dog. For most experts that clinches the argument in favor of the wolf.

There is also, of course, the fact that all you have to do is look at a German Shepherd or an Alaskan Malamute and think, "Wolf." But wait a minute. How do you get a Lhasa Apso out of a wolf? Well, there happens to have been a smallish, wooly wolf once found in large numbers in Tibet. It is also possible that there were kinds of wolves we simply don't know about.

Most important, it is very clear that dogs did not evolve on their own. Human beings intervened. A wolf cub is as cute as any dog pup, and there is a consensus that starting perhaps as little as fifteen thousand years ago primitive peoples started an experiment in breeding captured wolf cubs. The dog is not the result of Darwinian natural selection but of human beings deciding to breed for tameness and other qualities that led to a creature known as man's best friend.

2

So Many Different Breeds

Q: I get the impression that a couple of new breeds of dog are popping up every year. I assume that many of these are dogs that are well known in other parts of the world but that have only recently begun to become popular in the United States. *How many different breeds of dog are there?*

A: Allowing for some controversy as to whether certain breeds are really distinctive enough to be regarded as purebreds, there are certainly in excess of three hundred recognized breeds around the world. The majority of breeds were "set" during the final third of the nineteenth century, although there have continued to be new breed developments right down to the present. There are also a very considerable number of breeds that existed two hundred years ago that became extinct as separate types. Many of these were specialized hunting dogs that went out of favor as other breeds proved superior. In some cases these types were bred out of existence in the course of developing newer breeds, but in others they just gradually disappeared.

3

A Dog from Where?

Q: So many dogs have place-specific names, such as Boston Terrier, Irish Wolfhound, English Setter, Ibizan Hound. *To what extent does a place-specific name mean that the dog was indigenous to that particular place or area?*

A: There are very few dogs that can be said with certainty to have been indigenous to the particular area stated in or implied by their names, at least in the sense that they were there before being discovered by the rest of the world. Among these few is the Pekingese, which had been a royal pet in China for centuries before the British brought the first ones back to England after taking Peking in 1860. Another very ancient breed is the Lhasa Apso, which did not exist outside of Tibet until the 1920s, when they were first brought to England. On the other hand, the Ibizan Hound, although first discovered on that island off the east coast of Spain, was probably first brought there by the Phoenicians long before the birth of Christ. On the island they survived as a pure breed, while interbreeding eliminated them in the Middle East.

In most cases a place-name such as Boston or Ireland, for example, indicates that the dog was first developed there by cross-breeding. While we know a great deal about the kinds of dogs used to create the new breed in some cases, in others the line is considerably confused.

4

Dog Days of Summer

Q: I have heard several explanations of the phrase "the dog days of summer." Some people say it comes from the fact that when it is especially hot, dogs just lie around panting. I've also been told that the phrase was the invention of a Chicago newspaper editor in the early 1900s, based on the fact that news was so slow, space got filled up with dog stories. *Is there any certain derivation of the phrase "dog days of summer"?*

A: Actually the phrase goes all the way back to ancient Rome, but it wasn't connected to real dogs or their behavior. Rather, the Romans noted that the hottest days of the year were associated with the predominance in the night sky of the Dog Star, also called Sirius. Because the star is the brightest in the heavens, the Romans came to the conclusion that its heat must add to that of the sun. Thus they spoke of *caniculares dies,* literally "dog days."

5

From Working Dog to Pet

Q: Obviously there are a lot of dogs, like the Alaskan Malamute, the Border Collie, and various hunting dogs, that are more widely used as working animals than as pets. *Are there some breeds that have a harder time making the transition from working dog to pet?*

A: The distinction between working dog and pet has become increasingly blurred over the last century and a half. There are dogs that in rural areas may still be bred primarily as hunting dogs, while others of the same breed have been selectively bred for qualities particularly valued in a pet or a show dog. The degree to which careful breeding can change the nature of a breed over the years is dramatically illustrated by the English Bulldog. The breed was long used in England and Europe as a fighting dog, especially in the bloody spectacle of "bull baiting." During the early Victorian period, as the queen's emphasis on civility took hold, bull baiting came to be regarded as barbarous, and laws were passed against it.

Bulldogs had been so completely bred for this particular blood sport, however, that the breed was threatened with extinction, as had occurred with a number of highly specialized hunting dogs before it. Breeders were successful over the years in reversing the extreme aggression that had been developed in the Bulldog. From 1835 on a great effort was made to transform the fierce animal into a gentle one, and by 1873 the modern Bulldog was sufficiently established to be recognized by the Kennel Club of Great Britain. The contrast between their still-fierce appearance and their sweet-natured ways have endeared them to generations of dog lovers ever since.

6

Dog-Show Beginnings

Q: I'm aware that more of the modern breeds of dog were developed in Great Britain than anywhere else. *How far back were the first dog shows held in England?*

A: The first dog show in England, or anywhere else, was held in 1859. This relatively late date surprises many people, but there are good reasons for dogs to start being looked upon in a different way at this time—the Industrial Revolution was fully taking hold, trains had made it far easier for far-flung people to congregate in a central place, and, most important, there was less call for dogs to be regarded chiefly as working animals.

Dog shows quickly became popular, and within eight years the first attempt to set standards for individual breeds was made by a doctor named J. Walsh in a book called *The Dogs of the British Isles.* As the concept of such standards took hold, a need was seen for a national organization to oversee the various breed societies that had sprung up, and in 1873 the Kennel Club was established. The modern concept of the show dog was thus put firmly in place.

The Geography of
Pedigrees

Q: On a trip to France this past summer I visited with friends who had an Épagneul Picard, or Picardy Spaniel. I found it an absolutely beautiful dog with a wonderful disposition. It is recognized by the international dog federation known as the F.C.I. (headquartered in Belgium) but not by the American Kennel Club. *Are the reasons why some dogs are recognized by one official dog organization and not another basically a matter of geography, or do questions of breed standards enter into it?*

A: It is primarily a matter of the popularity and thus the number of dogs of a given breed in a particular country. The Picardy Spaniel is indeed a splendid dog, much favored by European duck hunters, but it is little known in America. Thus the Australian National Kennel Council recognizes the Large Munsterlander and the Shar Pei, which are not accredited by the American Kennel Club. The F.C.I. (Fédération Cynologique Internationale), founded in 1911, is a special case, since it recognizes all breeds from all major dog clubs around the world.

It should be said, however, that sometimes a breed, particularly one that has been recently developed, will be recognized by one organization and not another because of disagreements about pedigree. These usually get settled eventually if the breed becomes sufficiently common in a given country.

Show Me

Q: I was told by a proud show-dog owner that the great Westminster Dog Show held in New York each year is the oldest surviving sporting event held in the United States. *When was the first Westminster show held, and is it really the oldest American sporting event?*

A: The first Westminster show was held in May 1877, two years after the first Kentucky Derby. You will also get an argument from some groups of dog lovers about whether the Westminster show is really a sporting event rather than a beauty pageant. Such dog owners will say that the real sporting events for dogs are Obedience Trials, in which dogs must demonstrate their ability to obey commands and do the actual work for which they were bred. Dogs must be registered with the American Kennel Club to participate in Obedience Trials, but they do not have to conform to the exacting breed standards as to size, coat, and shape required at Westminster. They can even be altered, which would immediately disqualify a show dog.

There are quite a lot of owners who bridge the two

worlds, and you will find show champions at Obedience Trials as well as dogs that wouldn't have stood a chance in that more rarefied world. For the doggier kind of dog lover, Obedience Trials are regarded as the most fun to watch.

Naming the Purebred

Q: With the children grown, my husband and I are considering getting a purebred dog, one that we can enter for show at least on a modest level. We have been talking with some friends who have shown their dogs, and we understand that the fancy names under which purebreds are shown are chosen by the breeder. *Why doesn't the new owner get to choose the name for a purebred dog?*

A: It is a long-standing tradition that the breeder names the dogs in a purebred litter. This makes it possible to keep track of the lineage of successive generations of dogs in a clear-cut way. Thus one of the greatest of all Collies, way back in 1911, was called Ch. Seedly Sterling, sired by Parkside Pro Patria out of Ch. Seedly Sylvia, a dog sired by Ch. Seedly Special. (The *Ch.* stands for "champion" and is added to a dog's name once it has won a championship.) But that is simply the dog's official name. You can give it any unofficial name you want, from Alice to Zoe if it is a female, and Archie to Zeb if it is a male.

10

Tail Docking and Ear Cropping

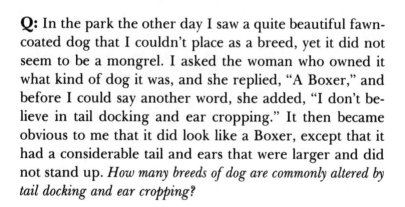

Q: In the park the other day I saw a quite beautiful fawn-coated dog that I couldn't place as a breed, yet it did not seem to be a mongrel. I asked the woman who owned it what kind of dog it was, and she replied, "A Boxer," and before I could say another word, she added, "I don't believe in tail docking and ear cropping." It then became obvious to me that it did look like a Boxer, except that it had a considerable tail and ears that were larger and did not stand up. *How many breeds of dog are commonly altered by tail docking and ear cropping?*

A: Far more than most people are aware. Ear cropping is not all that common, but is essential if one wants to show a Boxer, Great Dane, Doberman Pinscher, and a few other breeds. The procedure requires general anesthesia; not only are the ears cut to the "approved" shape, but they are also braced, to make them stand up. Ear cropping is usually carried out shortly after the puppy reaches three months, and the brace has to remain in place for several weeks. Many veterinarians simply refuse to perform this surgery these days, but others are sympathetic to the "show dog" ethos. Any owner wishing to have a dog's ears cropped should make certain that the veterinarian is fully informed of the dimensions required for a show dog.

Tail docking is much more widely practiced. About twenty percent of breeds recognized by the American Kennel Club are required to have their tails docked to be accepted for showing. The Spaniel, Terrier, and Pointer breeds, as well as Boxers, Poodles, Dobermans, and Weimaraners traditionally have their tails docked. This procedure is often carried out when the puppy is only a few days old, leading many owners to believe that the breeds are born with naturally short tails.

11
Sniff, Sniff

Q: Watching our Basset Hound sniff along the ground like a veritable detective, we wondered if the Basset has exceptionally good talents in the scent-tracking department, or does the dog's closeness to the ground compensate for a more ordinary sense of smell? *How much difference in the ability to detect scents exists between various breeds?*

A: There are wide differences between breeds. Generally hunting dogs are at the top, and toy breeds at the bottom. But any dog has a sense of smell that puts that of humans to shame. We have only about 500,000 receptors with which to record scents, while many breeds of dog exceed 100 million such cells. The Basset comes in toward the lower level for hunting dogs, with some 125 million receptors, but it is a very superior tracking dog due to a secondary advantage: As its long ears trail along the ground, they stir up the lingering smell from grass and dirt.

German Shepherds are in the top echelon of dogs when it comes to scent receptors, with 225 million of them to bring into play. This fact, together with their exceptional trainability, make them ideal dogs for policework and particularly for sniffing out hidden drugs.

12

That Lady Is a Bitch

Q: My husband and I both come from very straitlaced families. We want to get a dog, but would prefer a female because its sexuality is less obvious. But then we worry about our kids picking up the term *bitch. Is there anything wrong with calling a bitch a lady dog?*

A: Oh, come off it, or buy a goldfish.

The use of the word *bitch* to refer to a female dog has been around for six hundred years. It is impolite only when applied to a human female. And people have ways of getting around that. Remember how Barbara Bush, whose tale of her bitch Millie became a huge best-seller, referred to her husband's 1984 vice-presidential opponent as something that rhymed with "rich." Big wink. Enough. A female dog is a bitch.

13

Show-Dog Groups: Odd Tails

Q: The groups that various breeds of dog are assigned at dog shows seem confusing to me. Some groups have dogs that obviously belong together, but others seem almost haphazard. *How is the decision made as to what group a breed is assigned to in terms of showing?*

A: It is made by a committee of the American Kennel Club. There are six groups: Sporting Dogs, Hounds, Working Dogs, Terriers, Toy Dogs, and Nonsporting Dogs. There is a certain arbitrariness to the groupings, the main problem being that all six groups contain dogs that at one time were used as working dogs, although they may have done very different kinds of work. Even among the Toys, the Brussels Griffon was bred to work—as a rodent exterminator.

Some of the groups do make a good deal of sense. In the Sporting group, every dog was bred to do one (or more) of three things—to point, to flush game, and to retrieve. The Hounds are also hunting dogs, but they chase game, corner it, and keep it occupied until the hunter shows up. But while the Sporting group consists chiefly of four types— Pointers, Setters, Spaniels, and Retrievers—the Hound group is extremely varied—the contrast between an Afghan Hound and a Dachshund says it all, and to watch the two breeds competing against each other borders on the risible.

With Working Dogs things get even more miscellaneous, although most of them are large dogs, including Great Danes and Mastiffs, but the little Welsh Corgi is in there too. The Terrier group has in one sense the greatest consistency: They are all called Terriers, but they do what the Dachshund does—drive game into their holes and dig in after them. The Toy group also makes surface sense, since they are all very small. The only possible explanation for the Nonsporting group is that the dogs in it, from the Bichon Frise to the Poodle, didn't quite fit anywhere else. But we also have a renowned working dog, the Dalmatian, and a Terrier, the Boston, lumped in here too.

If it doesn't make sense, ask yourself what baseball's Atlanta Braves are doing in the National League West, or think about some of the nutty pairings they always seem to come up with for the Emmy Awards. Pigeonholing is a dirty job, but somebody has got to do it, and the American Kennel Club brooks no argument on its decisions.

14

The First Step Is Miscellaneous

Q: A friend is trying to talk me into buying a Jack Russell Terrier. This is not a breed that's recognized by the American Kennel Club. *What are the criteria for recognition by the A.K.C. and how long does it take?*

A: The first step is for the breed to be accepted into the A.K.C. Miscellaneous Class, with six to ten breeds carrying this status at any given time. To be accepted into the Miscellaneous Class, several criteria must be met. The breed must have been a distinct one for at least thirty years. Not only the number of dogs of the breed in the United States but also its geographic distribution come into play. Thus a specialized hunting breed localized in the Carolinas, say, would not qualify. A club devoted to the breed must exist, with a membership of at least one hundred. Each dog the club lists as registered must have a pedigree that goes back at least three generations, and there must be a comprehensive stud book for the breed.

Once accepted into the Miscellaneous Class, a breed will

be studied by the A.K.C. to make certain that there are no problems inherent in it. A breed is seldom given full A.K.C. accreditation in less than two years, but it may take far longer. In some cases the breed club's members actively resist full accreditation, especially in the case of working dogs that owners feel would suffer from the increased popularity that comes with A.K.C. recognition.

15

The Judging Elite

Q: The judges at dog shows obviously have a lot of power, in that the decision on winners rests with a single person. *How difficult is it to reach the point where a person is chosen to judge the Best in Show finale at a major show?*

A: A special license is required to be a Best in Show judge, and to reach that pinnacle of the dog-show world is at least as difficult—if not more so—as it is for a dog to win the coveted title the judge bestows. The world of judging is very political, especially when it comes to major shows, and there has been a good deal of agitation lately by people who feel that the top echelon of judges is a restricted club that makes it all too difficult to get into unless one has certain kinds of social or financial standing. There is a strong push to open up the judging ranks to greater num-bers of people, and while some reform of the process by which judges move up is likely, change is bound to occur slowly. Social standing has played a large part in the dog-show world from the very start.

16

American Kennel Club Debates

Q: At a recent dinner party an argument broke out about the American Kennel Club that verged on turning into a food fight. One male guest was doing the attacking. He was a gentleman farmer who raises Border Collies, which seemed to be at the heart of the matter. But he seemed to be angry across the board. *Why should the American Kennel Club be the subject of such a rancorous dispute?*

A: The American Kennel Club has been going through a rocky patch lately. It has been attacked for allowing indiscriminate breeding for profit without regard to standards, of permitting the "mutilation" of dogs to make them showworthy, of being controlled by an elitist eastern group centered on the Westchester Kennel Club, which sponsors the country's most important dog show, the Westminster, at Madison Square Garden, and of rigging the rules in such a way as to make it extremely difficult for new judges to win their credentials. Whew!

And it is certainly no accident that the outraged dinner

guest raises Border Collies. The Border Collie clubs have been fighting for years to avoid being brought under the umbrella of the American Kennel Club, on the grounds that the breed would be spoiled by the sometimes arcane standards that apply to the showing of recognized breeds. Many Border Collie owners and breeders cherish the individuality and rather broad spectrum of these wonderfully intelligent sheep-herding dogs and don't want to see the breed "prissyfied," as one critic puts it. They accuse the A.K.C. of making an end run around those who didn't want to have the breed recognized by encouraging the minority who do want recognition to form a splinter group.

Much of all this is politics. There are dog politics and cat politics, just as much as there are office politics and Washington politics. The A.K.C., however, has been sufficiently stung by some of the accusations that there are a number of reforms looming on the horizon.

17

The Other Club

Q: Friends have told me lately something about the United Kennel Club. *Is the United Kennel Club in direct competition with the American Kennel Club?*

A: Founded in 1898, the United Kennel Club, Inc., has had a different focus from the A.K.C., but there is little love lost between the two organizations. The U.K.C., based in Kalamazoo, Michigan, has long concentrated on Obedience Trials, but is taking steps to move toward more Confirmation Shows, which will inevitably put it more directly in competition with the A.K.C.

Since the U.K.C. has concentrated on dogs that still perform hunting or working tasks, they recognize only 160 breeds, as opposed to the 177 recognized by the A.K.C. The U.K.C. registers more than 225,000 dogs, the A.K.C. more than 1 million. One of the chief attractions of the U.K.C. to many dog owners is that it's more democratic and less "hoity-toity" than the A.K.C. While the activities of the two organizations overlap in several areas, there is no question that the larger club is far more powerful and a good deal more autocratic.

18

Top of the Charts

Q: A friend of mine claims that the Rottweiler is a more popular dog in the United States than either the Dachshund or the Beagle. They're beautiful dogs, but I find this assertion hard to believe. *Is the Rottweiler really one of the most popular dogs in America, and if so, what accounts for its status?*

A: The Rottweiler has been increasing in popularity for years and in 1990 climbed just ahead of the German Shepherd, into fifth place on the A.K.C. list of registered breeds. It is still outranked by the Cocker Spaniel, the Labrador Retriever, the Poodle, and the Golden Retriever. In seventh place is the Chow Chow, followed by the Dachshund, the Beagle and the Miniature Schnauzer.

Many owners are simply taken with the handsome looks of this 100-pound dog with its black coat and brown markings, but it is also a first-rate watch dog and a splendid family dog. The Rottweiler is extremely intelligent and highly trainable, although it requires an owner with a firm hand. Like almost all large dogs, it is excellent with children.

There has recently been controversy about a new "red"-coated strain of Rottweiler, which some Rottweiler enthusiasts believe is not a true purebred and is overly susceptible to health problems. There are those who disagree, but it seems wise to stick to the black standard at present. ———————

19

What's in a Mongrel?

Q: When asked what kind of dog I have, I reply that she is a cross-breed, with a lot of Border Collie, some Beagle, and probably some Terrier of one sort or another. But I've had people tell me that if there are more than two strains in my dog's genetic makeup, it's not a cross-breed but a mongrel. *Is there really a valid distinction between a cross-breed and a mongrel?*

A: Some experts maintain that there is a distinct difference. They like to point out that many dogs now regarded as purebred were "created" by careful cross-breeding. Thus they feel that the word *cross-breed* should be used to refer only to the offspring of two different kinds of purebred dogs. If one or both parents are themselves cross-breeds, then the resulting pups are mongrels.

The majority of experts, however, feel that this is just so much nit-picking, and use the terms *cross-breed* and *mongrel* without distinction. The term *mixed-breed* also has considerable currency. There are owners of dogs of uncertain heritage who dislike the word *mongrel*, feeling that it carries a degree of stigma. One man I know who likes to string people along always refers to his mongrel as "an American Domestic" and is delighted when someone asks if that is a newly developed breed.

20

Mutt Smarts

Q: The three dogs I grew up with (we always had two at once) were mongrels adopted from animal shelters. I'm now in my mid-twenties and have a mutt of my own. I get very annoyed when people ask what kind of dog I have and then turn up their noses because it isn't a purebred. *Isn't it true that mongrel dogs are often both healthier and smarter than purebreds?*

A: Many people believe that mongrels are smarter and healthier, on the grounds that purebreds are really "inbreds" and that the broader gene pool from which the mongrel derives is a good thing all around. Many veterinarians generally find that the mongrel dogs they have as patients are less prone to illness—although you won't hear them saying that to the owners of treasured purebreds.

On the other hand, this really isn't an assertion that can be proved. A mongrel may have the bad luck to have inherited a gene that predisposes it to certain problems too. And there is no question that there are some awfully dumb mutts as well as some exceptionally intelligent ones. At any rate no true dog lover will put down mongrels as a class. Unfortunately there are as many dog owners who are "keep-up-with-the-Joneses" types as there are car owners of the same ilk—and maybe more, since the whole concept of dog fancy grew out of middle-class aspirations to upper-class style during the Victorian period in England. Anyone interested in the degree to which social class played a role in the development of dog breeding should read Harriet Ritvo's very witty (and superbly researched) book, *The Animal Estate.*

21

Thinking About What Getting a Dog Really Means

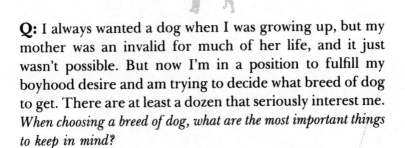

Q: I always wanted a dog when I was growing up, but my mother was an invalid for much of her life, and it just wasn't possible. But now I'm in a position to fulfill my boyhood desire and am trying to decide what breed of dog to get. There are at least a dozen that seriously interest me. *When choosing a breed of dog, what are the most important things to keep in mind?*

A: Here are several considerations that dog experts are virtually unanimous in recommending be given serious thought:

1. Do you have sufficient free time to really give the dog the intensive training it will need over the first few months if it is to be under control and happy? If not, you can look at the option of rescuing a mature dog from a shelter, but make sure it is not a dog that has been abused, which can require every bit as much attention as a puppy.

2. Will the circumstances of your life make it possible to see to it that the dog gets a proper amount of exercise? A dog that doesn't get enough exercise will be both unhappy and unhealthy. While all large dogs need a lot of exercise, there are many much smaller dogs that need a surprising amount. Read up on the exercise needs of any breed you are interested in.

3. Do you have young children? There are breeds that are terrific with children and others that are disasters. Be sure you know the difference.

4. Can you truly afford a dog? Take into consideration food costs, regular visits to the vet, possible kennel stays when you are away, and professional grooming for some breeds. And don't forget that dogs get sick or are injured. You need some emergency-fund leeway in your dog budget. A large dog can easily cost $2,000 a year to care for properly.

22

That Doggie in the Window

Q: There are four common sources from which to get a puppy: a friend or relative whose dog has had a litter, a pet store, a professional breeder, and the local animal shelter. *I've heard that pet stores are the least reliable source for a healthy dog, but are friends, breeders, or animal shelters really that much more likely to be the best bet?*

A: There are no statistics on this subject, but there is a great deal of talk, a lot of it contradictory. There are great success stories involving all four choices, as well as horror stories in regard to each. Pet stores do seem to take it on the chin more than the other three, but while there are too many pet stores that are supplied by "puppy mills" with dogs that are not up to par, there are also wonderful pet stores. Most experts don't like pet stores and recommend against using them unless you know someone who has gotten a good dog from the particular store. Impulse buying of the "doggie in the window" should be resisted no matter what.

But no matter what choice you make, you are taking some chances. If you get a puppy from a friend or relative, remember that the puppies in a given litter can vary a good deal even when both parents are purebreds, so don't turn on your old friend or cousin Jack if you end up with something of a dud. When it comes to breeders, it is again best to know someone else who has a strong, healthy dog from that source. There are many in the dog world who say that the best breeders are usually people who look upon what they are doing as an expensive hobby rather than as a business and that they are to be trusted most. But there are, of course, exceptions to every rule. And when it comes to animal shelters, you are obviously taking a spin at the roulette wheel, but you will also be doing a good deed. The best dog I ever had, a female Border Collie–Terrier mix, came from the privately supported Bide-A-Wee shelter in New York City.

23

Home Alone

Q: I grew up with dogs, but as a single adult with a small two-room New York City apartment, I am trying to make a decision between getting a cat and a toy dog. Since I work fairly long hours, I tend to think a cat makes more sense, but I really am a dog person. *Which of the toy breeds are least likely to have a problem about being left alone for fairly long periods?*

A: Whatever you do, stay away from Chihuahuas, which truly hate to be alone. (Since this breed is also jealous and doesn't like children, it is primarily a dog for retired people who are home a lot; it will reward being spoiled with great devotion.) Miniature Schnauzers seem to bear up quite well under circumstances where they are left alone a lot, but be sure to provide plenty of playthings and chew toys for their amusement. The ideal answer would be not one but two Japanese Chins. These are wonderfully amusing little dogs that take great delight in chasing each other around until they have worn themselves out to the point of needing a long nap. Extremely agile, they can race around like mad without ever causing any harm to furnishings or treasured objects.

24

Cat Compatible

Q: Our son, now ten, badly wants to have a dog. Each of his older sisters already has a cat. *Are there some breeds of dog that are more likely to fit into a household that is already cat-occupied territory?*

A: Successfully integrating a dog into a cat-occupied household will obviously depend as much on the cats as on the dog. But the fact that there is more than one cat may be helpful, since they are already dealing with the fact that the space must be shared. Dogs that are particularly good with animals of other species include Labrador Retrievers, Welsh Springer Spaniels, and, above all, Basset Hounds. Despite their considerable bulk and strength, Basset Hounds are real "pussycats" when it comes to temperament. They will even cope with a pet rabbit—despite the fact that they were originally bred to hunt rabbits!

25

Toy Terrors

Q: Our six-year-old son is begging us to get a dog. Since my husband's job has involved relocating every three or four years, we thought it might be best to get one of the toy breeds, since they are so easy to transport. I should add that I am pregnant, so there will soon be an even younger member of the family. *Are toy dogs a good bet as a family pet?*

A: Toy dogs, unfortunately, are very bad with children. They tend to be jealous and they have a pronounced aversion to any kind of rough play. Simply to protect themselves, they will snap at anybody who gives them even a minor tweak of the ear or tail. Toys can be wonderful pets for older people, especially those who live alone, since they are utterly devoted and easy to care for. But they are definitely not a pet for a growing family.

26

The Bigger the Better

Q: Our longtime next-door neighbors have moved away, and their house has been sold to some people we know casually. They are very pleasant, but because there is no fence between our yards, we worry about their dog. We have two children under five, and the new neighbors' dog is an absolutely huge Newfoundland. We're thinking of putting up a fence in a hurry. *Aren't very large dogs dangerous for small children to be around?*

A: Quite the contrary. The very large breeds are the most tolerant with children. Their very size makes them utterly unafraid, and they will put up with a great deal of teasing and roughhousing from young children. This is even true of the fearsome-looking Great Dane. Newfoundlands are famously wonderful with children, more so than any other dog except possibly the Old English Sheepdog, the breed immortalized as Nana in *Peter Pan*. Enlist your new neighbors in properly introducing your kids to their dog. You have nothing whatever to worry about.

27

Tricksters

Q: My eleven-year-old son has a real knack for working with animals. He's taught white mice to jump through hoops and go down slides, and thanks to his efforts we have a parrot with something approaching a Ph.D. in language skills. He wants a dog, and obviously it should be one with a particular aptitude for learning tricks. *Which dog breeds are regarded as the most trainable in terms of performing tricks?*

A: There are three breeds long associated with circus acts—the Pomeranian, the Poodle, and the Bichon Frise—any of which should "do the trick" for your son. Pomeranians have been great favorites of royalty, from Marie Antoinette to Queen Victoria, but they are subject to hereditary hip dysplasia—if you opt for a Pomeranian, seek out a breeder willing to guarantee that both parents were free from the problem. Poodles come in three sizes—Standard, Miniature, and Toy—and all three are fun-loving and affectionate. The little Bichon Frise, a flying powder puff of a dog, has been popular since the fourteenth century and may be the best acrobat of the lot.

28

A Traveling Companion

Q: I am a professional photographer specializing in nature scenes. As a result I travel a great deal by car. *Are there any breeds of dog that are particularly good travelers?*

A: Many of the hunting dogs are good travelers. The Dalmatian, bred as a coach dog, would be an even more obvious choice. But perhaps the best traveler around is the Welsh Corgi, of which there are two varieties, the Cardigan and the Pembroke. The Pembroke is the more popular, perhaps because of their long reign as the favorite of Queen Elizabeth II.

Small, only about a foot high and weighing just over twenty pounds, the Pembroke Corgi is nevertheless an excellent watch dog, but at the same time less suspicious of strangers than the Cardigan strain, which can overreact to intrusions into its owner's territory. Corgis need a good deal of exercise, but are not wanderers, liking to stick close to their owners. They are also very healthy dogs, unlikely to develop skin diseases, and robust in every way. A Corgi with a traveling owner who spends a lot of time outdoors would be a very happy dog.

29

Psychic Dogs?

Q: Over the years I have heard or read some astonishing stories about dogs that seemed to have a sixth sense— suddenly howling and trembling, for example, when an owner has been badly injured in a car crash miles away. *Do any experts believe that dogs can have psychic powers?*

A: Stories about "psychic" cats are much more common than similar accounts of dog behavior, perhaps because cats are inherently more mysterious than dogs. There are experts who do feel that there may be something to this idea in both cats and dogs, but skepticism abounds. Either sheer coincidence—which figures more extensively in our lives than many people like to admit—or natural explanations for extremely odd events are cited by most scientific observers in such situations. Human beings have amassed so much knowledge over the past several thousand years that we tend to forget how little we really know about the workings of our universe. While questions abound concerning the possibility of psychic behavior in animals, certainly the bond between some dogs and their owners goes beyond what can be fully understood.

30

The Allergic Dog Lover

Q: I am recently married. My husband grew up with dogs and would love to have one, but I am allergic to them. I have heard, however, that some people who are allergic to most dogs have found that certain breeds do not affect them. *Are there any particular breeds that are less likely to cause allergic reactions in people?*

A: Some allergic people find they do not have a problem with dogs that are very shorthaired, but that is not always the case. Allergic reactions in human beings are very complex and difficult to diagnose. I have a woman friend who was in your position who finally found two or three breeds that did not affect her, and only one of them was in fact shorthaired. What she did was make it a point to test herself in the company of a wide variety of dogs. If being close to them and petting them did not cause her to have an immediate reaction, she would spend additional time with a dog of that breed, either one owned by a friend or by actually visiting dog breeders. It was a process that took time and courage, but she and her husband are now the proud owners of a Boston Terrier.

31

Nonshedding Longhairs?

Q: I'm particularly fond of longhaired dogs, but most of them seem to shed dreadfully, leaving hairs all over the furniture. Recently I've seen advertisements for dogs like Lhasa Apsos and Shih Tzus stating that these breeds are nonshedding. *Is there really such a thing as a nonshedding longhaired dog?*

A: Such advertisements are extremely misleading, making a fundamentally false claim based on the difference between the ways different breeds shed their hair. Most longhaired dogs shed their coats on a cyclical basis, and when they do it, the hair sometimes seems almost to fly off their bodies. Dogs such as Lhasa Apsos don't shed on the same cyclical basis, and the hair does not drop off their bodies and clog the vacuum cleaner. But they do shed—inward toward the skin. If they are not regularly brushed to remove this dead hair, it will turn into a dense mat that often gets so tight and tangled that it can be removed only by shaving the dog virtually bald! Matting can also lead to skin lesions and infections. Thus a Lhasa Apso will in fact need *greater* attention paid to its coat than a longhaired dog that sheds outward on a cyclical basis.

32

Careless Breeding

Q: I keep hearing stories from friends and relatives across the country about having to put to sleep dogs of several of the most popular breeds at young ages because of various diseases. *Are most hereditary dog diseases the result of inbreeding?*

A: Inbreeding is part of the problem, but the real culprit is careless breeding. The more popular a given breed becomes, the more "puppy mills" spring up to keep pace with the demand. Indiscriminate, wholesale breeding can cause a genetic defect that exists in only a few dogs to become widespread very quickly. Some experts also point the finger at breeders of show dogs who put appearance ahead of all else, including health. The result is an increasing number of very popular breeds, including German Shepherds, Dobermans, Cocker Spaniels, and Rottweilers, that are in serious danger because of a diseased gene pool.

None of this has to happen. Increased knowledge of genetics and such tools as molecular biology should be producing more dogs that are free of genetic diseases; the reverse is occurring simply because there are too many careless, greedy breeders. There are, of course, responsible breeders. Their dogs are carefully screened before they are bred, and the resulting pups should be up to the highest standards of health. Do not hesitate to question a breeder very closely on the subject of the kinds and degree of genetic screening they employ.

33

Why Puppies Have Worms

Q: I gather that all puppies have to be dewormed. *Are most puppies born with worms, and if so, how do they become infected?*

A: The great majority of puppies are born with worms, which have been passed on to them by the mother. Roundworms are the most common intestinal parasite in dogs. But since roundworms usually do not affect an adult dog's health or cause diarrhea, the only way to know that a dog is infected is by microscopic examination of the stools. Even if the mother has been dewormed shortly before she became pregnant, she may pick up the parasite again. Thus puppies are routinely dewormed when they are five or six weeks old.

34

New Puppy Arrivals

Q: We're about to get a new puppy, and my husband and I—going by our childhood experiences—have different ideas about how much attention from our three children, two of them under six, is good for a puppy at the beginning. *Isn't it frightening to a puppy to have a lot of people, especially children, trying to play with it the minute it arrives at its new home?*

A: Yes. A new puppy, even one a few months old, is being asked to adjust to a great many new things at once, starting with the ride home. Its new surroundings, even a two-room apartment, are likely to seem vast in comparison with what the puppy is used to—do not be surprised if it decides to take shelter under a bed. Children should, of course, be allowed to touch and pat the puppy, but they must be told to be gentle at first and to hold down the noise level. If they protest, remind them how they wailed when too many relatives crowded around them when they were infants.

35

Rules for Children

Q: My son and daughter-in-law have two children, aged four and six, who engage in extremely rambunctious play with the family dog, a Newfoundland. The dog seems to be able to shrug off any amount of roughhousing and is genial and gentle to a fault. I suppose this should delight me, but I think it also has a downside. The children seem to be utterly unafraid of dogs in general, and I don't think they understand that a great many dogs are not anywhere near as docile, hardy, or patient as their own. I worry they will get hurt because of overconfidence. *Isn't it important to teach children that no matter how sweet their own dog is, they ought to be very careful with a strange dog?*

A: Absolutely. There are many breeds of dog that don't like children, many nervous or badly trained dogs, as well as breeds that are innately suspicious of strangers. Your grandchildren—all children—should be taught never to approach a strange dog that is off lead, never to try to pet even a leashed dog without asking the owner's permission first, and to pet a strange dog gently and without making any sudden moves. They should also keep their faces away from the strange dog—some dogs that will happily accept a pat or stroke from a child feel threatened when faces are thrust up against theirs.

36

Two Puppies to Train

Q: We have twin daughters who want not just a puppy but two puppies. Our daughters, most of the time, have proved a double delight, but I have the feeling that trying to train two puppies at once is likely to mean double trouble. *How difficult is it to train two puppies at once?*

A: Training two puppies at once does present some special problems. The main difficulty owners usually encounter is that when one dog is being disciplined, the other tries to horn in on the act and play disciplinarian too. There are no set rules for dealing with this problem, but extra firmness and patience are likely to be required.

Some experts suggest that if you're getting two puppies, it can help to take them home when they're a little younger than usual, say six or seven weeks. They may not learn quite as fast as an older puppy, but they are more malleable, allowing you to get a head start in other ways. Be sure to get two puppies from the same litter, so that you can observe the siblings playing together before making a choice. Given the fact that among human twins the older is often a little more aggressive, you may find that daughter opting for the most aggressive pup, while your other twin likes the more passive one. Don't allow that choice to be made, or you'll have greater problems. Try instead to get two pups that seem evenly matched in their behavior.

37

So Many Shots

Q: I was instructed by the breeder from whom I bought my Maltese that she will have to have a series of vaccinations over the next three to four months. *Is it really necessary for vaccinations to be spaced out over a period of months, or are all these successive visits to the vet some kind of boondoggle?*

A: A lot of dog owners, especially first-timers, get irritated by the number of trips to the vet required to vaccinate a puppy properly. But it has to be done this way in order to make certain that the dog is fully protected. A puppy initially receives a natural "vaccination" in the form of antibodies in the mother's milk. But it is unknown how long this protection really lasts, and the incubation periods of the various diseases involved are also not certain. Thus a series of shots is essential. Owners who try to get away with skipping one of these sets of shots are asking for trouble and much higher veterinary costs in the long run.

The shots administered are for canine distemper, hepatitis, and leptospirosis (all three usually combined into one shot called a DHL). Shots to immunize the puppy against parvovirus and parainfluenza, and of course rabies, are also essential. A dog should not be walked outdoors until its series of shots is complete at the age of four months or more.

38

Rabies Roulette

Q: We are on the verge of getting a puppy. Lots of people have been giving us advice (solicited and unsolicited). A woman in her sixties who lives down the street said that since we would be walking our new dog on a leash, there was no need to get rabies shots. In fact she insisted that rabies shots changed a dog's personality and that she had avoided them with her last three dogs. *Is there any truth to the idea that rabies shots are in some way detrimental to a dog?*

A: There have always been those who have made such claims, but they are virtually impossible to prove one way or another. Are any changes due to rabies shots or to the natural maturation of the dog? It's a chicken-and-the-egg dilemma. What is beyond dispute is that rabies is one of the nastiest diseases around, and that it is not an issue to play Russian roulette with. Louis Pasteur, who first used a rabies vaccine on a human being in 1885, was for a considerable time regarded as a monster by antivivisectionists, since the vaccine had originally been developed by deliberately infecting dogs. But the occasional outbreaks that occur even today are sufficiently horrifying to ensure that rabies vaccinations will go on being required by law. It is not a matter of choice, and to try to dodge having a dog vaccinated is asking for serious trouble.

39

Puppy Puddles

Q: My husband and I are having a dispute about house-training the nine-week-old mixed-breed puppy we just acquired. If we go out and come back to find that little Hillary has relieved herself anyplace other than her papers, my husband scolds her and pushes her nose down next to where she has soiled the floor. I say this doesn't do a bit of good and is just confusing to the dog. *Isn't it true that a puppy shouldn't be scolded or punished unless you actually catch it in the act?*

A: Yes. This is one area in which there is widespread agreement. A puppy simply will not understand what it has done wrong an hour after the event. One reason it is important that someone be in the house a lot of the time while training a puppy is to enable the owner to catch the dog in the process of relieving itself in inappropriate places. Scold the dog with a loud no or "Bad dog," and then take it to the place it should be using, whether it be papers or old cloths.

If you are wearing old clothes or are bare-legged, it can

be extremely effective to pick the dog up even as it is peeing and carry it to its papers. You will get dribbled on, but the puppy will usually be startled enough to shut off the flow. Put the puppy down on the papers and stay with it while it finishes the job. Then praise the dog for doing it right.

40

Tug-of-War Controversies

Q: We are having a family dispute about our six-month-old Boxer pup, which loves to play tug-of-war with our sons, who are eight and eleven years old. My husband thinks this is just fine, but my feeling is that we're encouraging bad habits. The puppy is very rambunctious in all ways, and I'm concerned about losing control of the training process. *Is it advisable to play tug-of-war with a puppy?*

A: There is a good deal of controversy about this subject. Some experts are adamantly against tug-of-war games, exactly because they believe it undermines discipline to allow a puppy to "fight" the owner for something. Some others think it is natural puppy behavior, but even they suggest the owner should encourage discipline by requiring the puppy to drop the object when the owner wishes the game to end. And, of course, if there is any sign of aggression by the dog, aside from a playful growl, the practice should be discontinued: A baring of the teeth, for example, cannot be tolerated.

In your own case I think the game should be stopped. Boxers can be stubborn and overly rambunctious, and they need a firmer hand during training than many dogs.

41

Bad Timing for a Bed

Q: We got our Terrier mix a dog bed when she was about seven months old. It was a wicker model with a soft cushion. To say that our Brenda did not take to it is putting it mildly—we came home one day to find that she had totally destroyed the wicker sides and back. *How can you tell what kind of dog bed a pet will take to?*

A: There are dozens of varieties of dog beds on the market, and the great majority will work just fine with most dogs. Your problem probably lies in the timing of introducing Brenda to a bed. Dogs enter a two- or three-month adolescence at about seven months of age, during which they suddenly start testing the rules and generally seeming to retrogress. It's best to get a dog bed once a puppy is sufficiently housebroken so that it will not soil its own "nest." The timing will vary from dog to dog, but you are at least three months too late. You can try again when your dog is just under a year, but stay away from wicker or wood, since terriers are renowned chewers.

42

A House of His Own

Q: My wife and I have just moved from the city to a suburban house with a large fenced yard. We want to get a dog, but because we have a lot of antiques, we feel it would be best to have the dog live primarily outdoors. Obviously we would want the dog to be happy and healthy and are trying to decide what kind of doghouse would be the best. We live in Alabama, if that is pertinent to the choice. *Are there certain kinds of doghouses that are regarded as superior?*

A: The number of doghouses on the market is extensive and diverse enough to border on the dizzying. The price range goes from under a hundred dollars to small mansions that cost several hundred. The main considerations should be a raised floor to protect your dog from dampness, a door or protective inner construction that will prevent drafts, ease of cleaning, and—in your case an important consideration—materials that are not hospitable to fleas. Your mention of antiques suggests that you might tend toward a wooden doghouse as a matter of taste, but in southern states the length and severity of the flea season clearly suggests plastic as much the better idea.

43

Consistency Is All

Q: Since we're about to get a dog, I've been looking at several dog-training books from the library. The more I read, the more confused I get; there seem to be so many different approaches. *Are there one or two approaches to dog training that are particularly successful?*

A: The reason there are so many differences of opinion on the best way to train a dog is that many of them are effective *for a particular owner with a particular dog.* Generally speaking, there are two main approaches, tough and tough-tender. But there are many creative variations within those categories. Read up on the breed you want to get. If you like a breed that is regarded as independent, stubborn, or demanding of an extra-firm hand, you should obviously be looking for a training approach in the tough category. If you don't feel that you have it in you to take a drill-sergeant approach, then you should probably look for a breed that is particularly responsive to training.

Remember that the most crucial aspect of training a dog

is consistency, so don't try using dog-training manuals as though they were Chinese menus, choosing one exercise from column A and another from column B. Select a training approach that fits your personality and that you feel comfortable with and you should do all right.

44

Too Much Praise?

Q: My brother-in-law, who has two hunting dogs, says that I praise my own Chow Chow too much for good behavior. His idea is that if circumstances changed and my dog had to get used to a somewhat different lifestyle, he would resist learning any new behaviors. *Is it possible to give a dog too much praise for good behavior?*

A: There is some dissension among dog experts on this issue. At one end of the spectrum there are those who say that a dog should receive about eight to ten times as much praise as it does corrective orders. Other experts feel that is considerably overdoing it and can lead to spoiling a dog. Much of the difference in approach here seems to arise from the kind of existence a dog is being trained for. Thus owners who are involved with working dogs, whether they are used for hunting, guarding, policework, or herding, tend to put a greater emphasis on the obedience end of things. All dogs require considerable praise if training is to be effective, though many people who own working dogs like to keep a tighter rein than owners whose dogs are simply pets. One reason why many owners of show dogs employ someone else to train and handle the dog in the show ring is that the owner finds it difficult to be firm enough.

It should also be noted that some breeds need a stronger hand than others. The Chow Chow is among these breeds. But ultimately each owner and each dog have a unique relationship. If your own dog is well behaved, you must have gotten past the willfulness that Chow Chows can exhibit, and in that case whatever you are doing apparently works.

45

Backing Up the Tone of Voice

Q: I've been hearing lately about some dog-training programs that emphasize the owner's body language. I always thought that tone of voice was the crucial element. *Is body language anywhere near as important as tone of voice when training a dog?*

A: Some trainers have been placing a new emphasis on body language lately, but not as a substitute for tone of voice. It is just that dogs are acutely attuned to body language, more than many owners realize, and that if the tone of voice is not backed up by appropriate body language, the dog receives conflicting signals. Once again, the real crux of the matter is consistency, and tone of voice and body language should be in sync. In addition, by paying more attention to body language, owners can add another string to their repertoire of commands, so that in certain situations, for example, a sharp shake of the head can bring your dog under control even without a verbal no.

46

A Way with Dogs

Q: Our much-loved Dachshund is also a little devil some of the time, mischievous and stubborn as all get out. Sometimes we are amused, sometimes decidedly not. A very close friend of ours, a woman in her late thirties who had dogs as a child but hasn't had a pet in many years, has an effect on our Gertrude that is extraordinary. Gertrude will do absolutely anything our friend tells her to, after having totally ignored our commands. *When a nonfamily member can get your dog to behave better than you can, is it because the friend is in fact around less often or is it because the friend has some sort of special gift?*

A: Your friend almost certainly has a natural gift for dealing with dogs. I have seen the same thing happen many times. Anyone who loves dogs has some of this gift—dogs require vastly more time, patience, and empathy than cats do, which may be why cats have become more popular—but some individuals simply have a special ability to connect with dogs. They would make wonderful dog trainers, but they are very often successes in utterly different fields. You may be astonished when a friend who is a bank officer or advertising writer effortlessly establishes control over your dog, but your dog has probably sized up the situation almost instantly. It's a gift some people have.

Name That Squeak Toy

Q: My dog has half a dozen different squeak toys. Every time I give her a new one, I give it a name, and I use the name fairly often when playing with her. The result of this is that I can ask her to bring me a particular toy out of three or four scattered around the room, and she will pick it out and carry it to me in her mouth. Some of my friends think this is just wonderful and are very impressed, while others insist that I must be using my voice in such a way or employing some kind of body language that gives Liza a clue, and that she can't really know all the different names. *How many different words can a dog understand and can they make a distinction between objects on the basis of just a name?*

A: It is certainly possible that your Liza is indeed making a clear distinction between her toys on the basis of the names you have given them. But that makes her an exceptionally intelligent dog. There is some disagreement among experts on this subject, but many believe that dogs are capable of understanding as many as fifty different words. This is unusual, however; the great majority of dogs grasp only about a third as many words. The ability to understand a considerable number of words seems to be particularly strong among breeds originally developed for sheep herding, but Poodles can also be remarkable in this regard.

48

Not Quite Fetching

Q: There's something I've noticed about dogs that I find quite curious. When most dogs play "fetch" with their owners, they refuse to bring the thrown stick all the way back, dropping it just out of reach. Obviously some dogs can be trained to bring it all the way back, since I've seen it done, but it's clearly unusual. *Why do most dogs resist bringing a thrown stick all the way back?*

A: Most dog owners assume they're being teased, but there is more to it than that, as the poet, English professor, and professional dog trainer Vicki Hearne explains in her splendid book on the relations between humans and animals, *Adam's Task*. The first time a stick is thrown for a puppy to fetch, Ms. Hearne notes, "Fido is fairly likely to bring it all the way back. The second time, however, Fido typically says, 'Well this is fun and all that, but can I trust her with *my* stick?' So Fido compromises by bringing the stick to a point just out of reach and dropping it there so that the human, if she wants to play fetch, must accept this modified version and pick up the stick herself."

All dogs are resistant to bringing the stick all the way back; training a dog to do so is one of the more difficult tasks faced in the course of bringing a dog up to snuff as a retriever.

49

Car Chasing

Q: My Collie has a bad habit of chasing motorcycles and cars with noisy mufflers. *How can a dog be stopped from chasing cars?*

A: The dog should be kept in a fenced yard and should not be allowed off its lead under any circumstances. No dog, in fact, should ever be off lead unless it has been trained to stop instantly if told to do so. Unfortunately many car-chasing dogs don't give up this bad habit until they have been hit by one—and then it may be too late.

50

The Obedient Owner

Q: I have a rather large mixed-breed (there's certainly some Labrador in him) that I've been having problems with in terms of obedience. When I take him for a walk, he is very difficult to control and only rarely pays the slightest attention to commands such as "heel" or "sit." Smoky is almost a year old, and it's clear I need help in getting him to obey, but my budget can't really withstand private training sessions, and I've talked to a number of people who say that group obedience classes just haven't worked for them. *Are group obedience classes really just a waste of time?*

A: Group obedience courses for dogs can work, but they do have a very high "dropout" rate, often exceeding 50 percent. Owners complain that they don't get enough (or any) personal attention and that their dogs aren't learning anything. These complaints are sometimes justified, but owners often fail to understand what obedience classes are really about. The main learning in an obedience class must be done by the *owner,* not the dog. It is not just to be cute that many obedience classes pass out "diplomas" at the conclusion of the sessions (which can last from eight to ten weeks) certifying that the owner has "graduated," with no mention of the dog's name.

The owner who enrolls in a dog-obedience course must do his or her homework, practicing regularly throughout the period between classes. The owner is being taught what to do and how to do it; he or she must then apply what has been learned to teach the dog. To find a group class that can be successful for you, ask to monitor a class (without your dog). As you observe the session, ask yourself, "Can *I* learn from this instructor?" When you find a class led by someone whom you feel *you* are comfortable with, you are likely to find that a group obedience course can indeed work for you, and thus ultimately for your dog.

51

Dogfight Dos and Don'ts

Q: There is a dog in our neighborhood that has a tendency to go after other dogs. So far we have avoided problems, but feel uneasy about the situation. *Are there some particularly recommended ways for breaking up a dogfight?*

A: If two dogs that are both on leads go after each other, really hard jerks on the lead by both owners may work. When both dogs are loose, there is not much you can do unless you have water handy. A bucket of water thrown on the dogs may work, but a hose is more effective. Under no circumstances try to separate the dogs with your bare hands, or you are likely to be severely bitten. In almost all cases of ordinary dogfighting (as opposed to illegal betting fights in which dogs are [mis]trained to go for the kill), one dog will submit and the fight will be over. Get any wounded dog to a vet immediately.

52

Private Training for Problem Dogs

Q: Our mixed-breed puppy is adorable but shy around both people and other dogs. (She was the "runt" of the litter.) We want to enroll her in obedience classes and are trying to decide whether a group class or private training is preferable. *Will a shy dog be overwhelmed in a group class, or would the experience be beneficial?*

A: The majority of dogs do quite well in group classes, which are of course less expensive. But the experts are pretty much in agreement that the group experience is not for very shy dogs or overly aggressive ones. The former can indeed feel overwhelmed, and the latter are too disruptive. Take your time in deciding on a trainer for private classes, however—it's very important that he or she have a real rapport with your puppy. Some trainers are more adept at dealing with aggressive dogs than they are with shy ones. This situation is one case in which it is wise to let the dog do the choosing, as it were. Your dog doesn't need a drill-sergeant type, but rather a friend. There's an equivalent human situation here. Every summer camp for kids has at least one counselor who was hired because he or she is especially adept at dealing with the children who wish they weren't there in the first place. There are dog trainers with high empathy quotients, too, and that's what your dog needs.

53

The Prodigal Dog

Q: Our two-year-old Irish Setter is a wonderful dog except for one thing: He runs away every few months. Once he got as far away as the next town, where some nice people took him in and called us (he has a tag with our number). But usually he comes home on his own, sometimes after many hours, sometimes not for a day or two. We're so glad to see him when he gets back that we haven't the heart to punish him, but maybe we're making a mistake. *Should runaway dogs be punished when they arrive back home?*

A: No, they shouldn't. They may not understand what the punishment is for, and it could even lead to a dog staying away longer for fear of being punished. Of course if you can catch him as he's taking off for the horizon, that's another matter. Dogs that run away are often hunting breeds, like your Irish Setter, and some experts suggest that it is their hunting instinct that causes them to roam. It might seem that the obvious solution is to tether your dog in the yard, but in fact that is likely to make him even more frustrated and unhappy. Some dogs with runaway tendencies stop doing it as they get older, and the fact that you greet yours with affection when he returns may help to curb the behavior.

54

The Lonely Barker

Q: We have accepted the gift of a Beagle puppy from friends (the litter has just been born, so we won't be getting it for eight weeks). In the meantime we've been told that Beagles tend to bay when they are left alone. Our neighborhood has a lot of retirees living in it, so a noisy dog just won't do. *How difficult is it to teach a Beagle not to bay when left at home by itself?*

A: Beagles do have a carrying bay that can disturb neighbors, but excessive barking when the owner is absent can be a problem with many breeds of dog. Essentially the dog is protesting about being left alone, which means that it has to be taught that the owner is inevitably going to be absent on a regular basis and that barking will not be tolerated. Such barking must be curtailed as soon as it begins to occur. Too many owners think it's terribly cute that little Bowser is yapping away when he first finds his voice and then discover that the barking has become a habit.

The most common method of breaking this habit is the "pop-back-in" ploy. Leave, going far enough away so that the dog thinks you are indeed "deserting" it, then turn around and go back home. Puppies will usually continue to bark until you are back in sight, even if they have heard you coming. Scold the dog, leave again, and come back again. This will have to be repeated several times over several days and requires patience (and an adjustment in your scheduled time to get to work, say), but it must be done. Then when you leave and hear no barking, go back and praise the dog and reward him. If a puppy stops barking just before you get back, leave and wait again. The dog must not get the idea that barking brings you back *except* to scold it, but rather that only silence will be praised.

For dogs that are problem barkers (usually because the proper training has been left too late), there are collars on the market that respond to the vibrations of barking and deliver a mild shock to the dog. But don't get one of these unless you really have a problem. The process of training a dog not to bark when you leave brings valuable dividends in many other areas of training. Don't be lazy; take charge yourself.

55

To Bathe or Not to Bathe

Q: My Cocker Spaniel has a wonderfully tawny and silky coat. I like to keep it looking that way, but I've been told that it is not good to bathe dogs too often. *What length of time should pass between one bath and the next to keep a dog's coat looking its best?*

A: A Cocker Spaniel, like other long-coated dogs, can be bathed every month or six weeks, but not more often since the dog's skin needs time to replenish its natural oils. The answer would be completely different for other breeds of dog. A friend of mine had a Labrador Retriever that was never bathed in its life. Its short, oily coat needed nothing more than brushing. Dogs that have undercoats, from Schnauzers to Komondors, should not be bathed more than twice a year at most. They are very difficult to bathe properly, with soap residue one problem and proper drying of the undercoat another.

Whether you bathe a dog in a shower, tub, sink, or outdoors, it is very important that the atmosphere be warm and that the dog be thoroughly dried—dogs are extremely susceptible to drafts when they are wet. Mild shampoos should be used, either baby shampoo or a specially formulated dog shampoo. Be very careful about the dog's eyes, which are easily irritated.

Flea infestations may make more frequent bathing essential. And show dogs are, inevitably, bathed more often than most experts feel is good for a dog. But except for water-loving hunting dogs—which are bred to withstand cold—moderation is certainly the best course when it comes to giving dogs a bath.

56

Grooming Disputes

Q: I have just had a rather nasty argument with the owner of a dog-grooming salon. My Chow looks more as though she had been attacked than groomed, but the owner says it is entirely my fault because the dog is so badly behaved. I admit she is a handful, but that's exactly why I take her to be professionally groomed in the first place. *Should a dog groomer really be in business if he or she can't handle "difficult" dogs?*

A: This is, I fear, rather a hairy problem. While your anger is understandable, it may be that you are expecting too much. Whether it is a matter of grooming humans or animals, this is not an area in which the old sales maxim, The customer is always right, pertains—as the comic-strip character Cathy constantly discovers to her chagrin. The courts have sometimes been caught up in disputes about grooming, and they tend to favor the groomer. After all, no guarantee has been made.

Many people have found that their "difficult" dogs will behave for a certain groomer and not for others. In that case you can insist that the particular person on the staff who seems to know how to soothe your dog into relative calm must be the one assigned to the task. But we all, dogs and humans, have bad days, and a bad haircut is really one of life's lesser problems.

57

A Summer Haircut?

Q: I have a friend who shaves the outer coat of his shaggy mixed-breed for the summer in order to help the dog stay cooler. This seems to me to be interfering with Mother Nature. *Is it wise to shave the outer coat of a dog for the summer months?*

A: It may be okay with some dogs in very hot areas, but it's something to think twice about. If the dog spends any length of time outdoors on a daily basis, it seems unwise in that it allows the sun's ultraviolet rays to penetrate through to the skin. Dogs can get skin cancer too. In addition, while it may seem illogical, the outer coat, especially if the hair is light-colored, can serve to bounce some of the heat off the dog, thus protecting it rather than making it hotter.

58

Skunk Encounters

Q: Since we live in a semirural area, we can allow our Springer Spaniel to run loose as he pleases. Unfortunately he has a tendency to find skunks far too interesting for his own good. *Is there any way to help get rid of skunk odor fairly quickly?*

A: There is a partial remedy to skunk odor that I first encountered when I was a kid. I was visiting relatives on a farm, and one of their dogs had an encounter with a skunk. My fourteen-year-old cousin knew exactly what to do. He went to the kitchen and got a couple of large cans of tomato juice, with which he washed the dog out by the barn. Then he gave the dog a second bath with soap and water. This procedure was repeated again the next day. It didn't completely remove the odor—it took several days to dissipate entirely—but it helped enough to make the dog bearable company. Why does it work? Nobody knows.

59

All Dressed Up and No Place to Show

Q: Our poodle, Nancy Drew, is a wonderful creature, but even though she has the proper papers, we have never considered showing her. We think some of the fancy haircuts we see on poodles at dog shows verge on the silly. *Is there any reason why a poodle shouldn't be allowed to have a full coat of hair?*

A: Of course not. The accepted style of cut for show dogs has changed several times over the past hundred years anyway. You should, however, keep Nancy Drew well trimmed. No breed has a faster-growing coat than poodles do, and quite aside from looking unkempt when they are not clipped regularly, hair that is too thick can lead to various skin problems. But by all means let her wear a "natural" look.

60

Neutering Notions

Q: One of my cousins is a strong animal-rights activist. I share some of her concerns, but in her zeal I think that sometimes she overstates matters, and some of her views seem contradictory. For example, while she does not believe that any dog or cat should be put to sleep by animal shelters unless it is gravely ill, on the other hand she insists that spaying a bitch or castrating a male dog is cruel. In support of this latter statement, she claims that neutered dogs become "a different animal." *How much is a dog affected in ways other than its ability to reproduce when it is neutered?*

A: The idea that neutering causes dogs to change considerably in other ways is a myth, but it's been repeated for so long that it is difficult to eradicate. Dogs do not get fat or lethargic after being neutered. They do not change their basic personalities. And a hunting dog will retain all its instincts in that regard.

There are dog owners who insist that it is "unnatural" to neuter a dog—even though the same owner has no intention of allowing the dog to mate, which is in itself an "un-natural" situation. Some owners even pack their bitches off to a kennel when they are in heat, to prevent mating, to avoid the spotting of rugs and furniture that can occur from vaginal discharge and, I sometimes suspect, to save themselves from watching the misery their dogs often go through. The "logic" involved here seems to me to border on the perverse. Such dogs should be spayed.

61

When to Spay

Q: Some dog owners I know say that a female dog should be allowed to go through several heats before being spayed, because otherwise her "personality" will not be fully developed. Others say that early spaying can prevent problems such as cancer of the mammary glands. *Does early spaying really cut down all that much on the possibility of cancerous tumors in female dogs?*

A: Yes, early spaying greatly lowers the possibility of mammary cancer. Only skin cancers, which also affect male dogs, have a higher incidence than mammary tumors. Many bitches develop noncancerous lumps, but the chance of malignancy is over 40 percent when such tumors develop in unspayed females.

As to the matter of underdeveloped "personality" in spayed dogs, you are dealing with the same kind of prejudice that leads some people to say a woman who doesn't have children isn't a "whole woman." The majority of veterinarians these days will recommend that spaying take place before the female dog even has her first heat so that the bitch's system is spared the shock of having an already developed hormonal flow cut off. The more heats the bitch goes through before spaying takes place, the greater the disruption.

62

No Tales of Conquest

Q: Several of my buddies are appalled that I'm considering having my ten-week-old Pointer castrated. How would *you* like it, they ask. I'm not interested in breeding the dog, and I don't want to be even accidentally responsible for adding to the dog overpopulation figures. *But aren't there also several health and behavioral reasons for having a dog castrated?*

A: There certainly are. It will make it far less likely that your dog will get into fights with other males. It will prevent the dog from mounting furniture and people. Your dog will make a better companion in general, since it will have its mind on you and not on other dogs—males to fight and females to mount—down the street. And from a health standpoint, castration will prevent such conditions as prostate enlargement and tumors of the testicles.

A dog that is castrated around the twelfth week will never know what it is "missing." Dogs don't hang out in locker rooms exchanging tales of conquest.

63

Early Neutering

Q: My sister, who lives in California, recently adopted a puppy from an animal shelter. The puppy was less than eight weeks old, but it had already been neutered when she got it. I'm all for neutering dogs to cut down on the vast numbers of unwanted animals that have to be destroyed every year, but is it really medically sound to do the surgery at such a young age. *Is the neutering of very young dogs safe?*

A: There is a lot of controversy about neutering dogs that are only a few weeks old, but the practice is becoming more common at animal shelters in several states. There is a good reason for doing it. Many animal shelters make new owners pay a neutering fee before a dog is taken home, advising that the dog should be brought back for the surgery in five or six months, depending on the sex of the dog. But even though the procedure has been already paid for, as many as half the owners fail to follow through. By doing the neutering very early, animal shelters have found that the number of unwanted puppies thrust upon them goes down very considerably.

Veterinarians are, however, seriously divided on the practice of early neutering. Proponents claim that not only is there no increase in the number of dogs that die during surgery (which is small anyway), but that the younger puppies recover more quickly from the operation. The skeptics worry that side effects may crop up down the line, even years later. These vets want to see reliable follow-up studies of dogs that have been neutered early before they will go along with the idea.

64

Canine Birth-Control Pills

Q: We have a pedigreed female Maltese puppy. We'd like to see how she turns out and retain the option of breeding her farther down the line. On the other hand we know that a bitch in heat is not a very happy creature, and we've been wondering about the use of canine birth-control pills we've heard about. *Do canine birth-control pills work and are they safe?*

A: There are two such pills on the market now, and others are under development. But there are drawbacks to them, in terms of both practicality and health. In practical terms, figuring out when to give them can be a problem. And both pills have a range of side effects. Veterinarians don't like to see them used for more than four or five heats, which would give you a couple of years to make up your minds about breeding your bitch. Some bitches, however, are far more affected by these drugs than most, and permanent reproductive problems can result.

65

Signs of Pregnancy

Q: Our sixteen-month-old Irish Setter got loose recently while she was in heat. We are not certain whether or not she was mounted by a male before we rounded her up. *How soon can you tell if a bitch is pregnant, and what are the telltale signs?*

A: You are going to have to be patient. In small and very slender breeds, a veterinarian may be able to confirm a pregnancy by feel after three weeks, but a month is more likely, and since Irish Setters are fairly large, it could easily be even longer than that. Thus the first definite sign of pregnancy may be the beginning of enlargement in the bitch's teats; at first they will also harden, then soften and become even larger. Teat enlargement generally begins at around five weeks. It will be another month, varying by a day or two, before she gives birth.

66

Pregnancy and Appetite

Q: As a recent first-time mother, I experienced a lot of fluctuations in appetite during my pregnancy. Now our Collie is pregnant. I assume similar things will happen to her. *Is there any rule of thumb about the changes in appetite a bitch will undergo during pregnancy that will make it possible to judge how much food to give her?*

A: Studies have found that there are changes not just during pregnancy but also during her heat. A drop in food consumption is often common during heat and will continue if the dog is impregnated. By the end of the ovulation period food intake increases for a couple of weeks during the start of gestation and then drops again briefly. From the fourth through the seventh week of pregnancy, food consumption may be as much as 40 percent above normal. Your dog will know what it needs, so during a heat and just afterward put out the usual amount of food and don't worry if it isn't fully consumed. Then start increasing the amount of food made available, little by little.

When the bitch suddenly starts leaving food, still continue to put out the same amount, because the period of appetite loss can vary by as much as a week.

During the fourth through eighth week gradually increase the amount of food. Remember that the abdominal cavity is being filled with the growing fetuses, however, and try giving smaller meals more often as the weeks pass. A sharp drop in food intake or even total refusal of food in the ninth week means that birth is imminent.

Stagestruck Lizzie

Q: Our Cairn Terrier bitch will be whelping soon. We have been told that we may have to persuade her to spend sufficient time with her puppies, since Cairn Terriers are so attached to their owners that they would rather be with them than with their pups. *How much time do most bitches spend with their newborn puppies?*

A: The amount of time varies a lot from breed to breed and even within a breed. Many bitches will want to be around the puppies a great deal of the time at first. Still, I once knew a Labrador-Newfoundland mix that was performing in a summer-theater production of the musical *Camelot*, playing the important role of King Pellinore's faithful companion. It wasn't discovered until a week into the month-long run that the stagestruck Lizzie was pregnant, and the only understudy that could be rounded up was a rather small dog not properly suited to the role. During the final week of the run Lizzie went home and gave birth two hours after the performance. It seemed likely that the poor understudy would have to go on the next evening, but at the time Lizzie usually departed for the theater, she pushed open a screen door and started barking at the car. Her owner dutifully delivered her to the theater. The show must go on!

This was an unusual case, to say the least. Most new mothers will spend quite a lot of time with their puppies during the first month to six weeks, but there are bitches that are likely to try to spend less time with them than they should. A Cairn Terrier is indeed one of those breeds likely to want to be with its owners as much as possible. In such cases it may prove necessary to sit with the bitch at least while she is nursing.

68

An Incomplete Creature

Q: I understand that puppies are considerably less developed at birth than human babies. *Exactly how helpless is a newborn puppy?*

A: Very. The puppy is blind, deaf, and has limited motor ability. It can suck and it can crawl a little. Many people are astonished to learn that a newborn puppy does not even have elimination reflexes. The mother must lick the puppy in order to stimulate elimination. A puppy will open its eyes after two or three weeks, and in the third week it also begins to hear. You will notice that it becomes startled at various noises.

From three weeks of age on, things begin to happen very quickly. The baby teeth will begin growing in during the fourth week and the puppy will be able to walk. Weaning is usually completed by six weeks of age, and the puppy will be able to ingest solid food.

In some dogs there is also a considerable difference in appearance between a newborn puppy and an adult dog of the breed. For example—as devotees of Disney's *101 Dalmatians* will be aware—Dalmatian puppies are solid white at birth. The spots do not even begin to appear until after the second week. Thus in many ways a newborn puppy is very much an incomplete animal.

69

Hungry Pups, Hungry Mothers

Q: Obviously a nursing mother will need more food and water. But I have heard widely divergent amounts mentioned. *Does the extra amount of food and water needed by a nursing mother vary pretty much according to the size of the breed, or is it more complicated than that?*

A: The new mother probably won't eat anything for twenty-four hours. She will, after all, be busy digesting the afterbirth (those who want their children to witness the "miracle of birth," please take note and prepare them for this). The amount of food and water required after that can vary according not only to the size of breed but also to the number of puppies in the litter, and even with dogs of the same breed there can be considerable differences. The mother will certainly need as much as two times her normal consumption of food and water and may require four times as much. It's better to put out too much food at the beginning and judge by how much is being left behind over the first few days. The lactating mother will need the additional amount for at least three weeks and often up to four.

A Full Menu

Q: I'm a widower nearing sixty and have decided to get a dog for companionship. My family had a dog when I was growing up, but that was a long time ago, and I haven't had one since for a variety of reasons. I recall that back in my youth Crosby, an Irish Setter, was fed a mixture of dry dog food and cooked innards, such as heart, that my mother got at the butcher shop. Looking at the long aisle of dog foods in today's supermarkets, I find myself somewhat bewildered. *Are there any general rules about the best kind of dog-food diet?*

A: There is indeed a vastly larger amount of choice when it comes to dog food now than there was in your youth, and for once it can be said that with greater choice there has also been a real improvement in quality. Over the past fifteen years nutritional studies of dogs of all kinds, sizes, and ages has led to an understanding of what dogs need to consume that in many ways outstrips what we know about the considerably more complicated human body.

Basically there are four types of dog food: dry, semimoist, canned "rations," and canned meat foods. Within each of these categories there are also products targeted for various age groups, from rambunctious puppy to sleepy old hound. The first distinction to be noted among the four categories is cost. Dry dog food is the least expensive, canned meat foods the most costly. All are carefully balanced nutritionally, and people with only modest means or several dogs quite naturally tend to choose dry food. But even though any of the four categories will assure the general good health of your dog, there are differences between them.

Dry food is not only cheap but also can be put out without danger of spoiling, particularly if the food is not subsequently moistened, having plenty of water on hand in a separate bowl instead. Dry dog food is also good for the gums and helps to some degree to cut down on tartar buildup on the teeth. Some dogs, however, especially small ones, may have problems digesting dry food.

Semimoist food, in packets, does not have to be refrigerated even after opening, and some dogs find it more palatable than dry food. When it comes to canned dog foods, some dog owners are not fully aware of the differences between the canned-rations type and the more expensive meat type—the ration type contains barley, meat by-products, wheat grain, and soy flour, whereas the meat type has meat by-products, meat, poultry by-products, and soy flour. You get what you pay for.

Some dogs seem to be born "picky" and won't have anything to do with any type except canned meat. Many experts suggest a mixture of two or more kinds and occasional table scraps, but in the end price, convenience, and the preferences of a given dog are all likely to be factored in to the chosen diet.

71

Special-Purpose Dog Foods

Q: As a lifelong dog owner now in my sixties, I have greeted with suspicion the introduction in recent years of dog foods that are supposedly targeted to the age of the dog or special circumstances such as pregnancy. These new products are higher priced, and I can't help but wonder if they are more a matter of advertising than real nutritional advance. *Are specially targeted dog foods everything they are cracked up to be?*

A: It's difficult these days not to wonder if *any* commercial product is everything it's cracked up to be. But knowledge about the nutritional needs of dogs has enormously increased in recent years as the result of far more stringent and complex testing programs. The new lines of dog food take advantage of this information, and they take a lot of the guesswork out of feeding a dog properly as it ages or under special circumstances. They are more expensive because they require greater attention during production and because they do not sell as widely as the older all-purpose brands. Someone with a lot of experience with dogs, like yourself, may not have much need for these products; you've probably long since learned how to make adjustments in diet on the basis of acquired knowledge. For the less-experienced dog owner, however, special-purpose foods can be both useful and reassuring.

72

A Shiny-Coat Diet

Q: Joe, our six-year-old Cocker Spaniel, used to have a wonderfully shiny coat, but he was getting a bit heavy and we changed his diet, giving him a mixture of canned and semimoist food instead of only canned. *What nutritional aspect of a dog's diet is particularly responsible for a shiny coat?*

A: The shininess of a dog's coat, which in the show-dog world is referred to as "bloom," is affected by the amount of fat in the dog's diet. For that reason many show dogs are fed several times as much fat as the minimum requirement of 5 percent of the daily diet. But show dogs are under a good deal of stress, and they burn off the extra calories that fat contains more easily than the ordinary house pet. Moreover, they are young dogs, whose careers are usually over by the time they are four or five years old, after which the amount of fat in their diets is normally reduced.

Since canned dog food contains as much as three times the fat content of semimoist, the new mixture you are feeding Joe is providing him with considerably less than his body is used to getting. If you wish to increase the fat content, you will have to decrease the amount of food in order to promote weight loss. For dogs as for humans, something has to give in the diet in order for weight to be lost, either quantity or caloric value.

73

Postprandial Strolls

Q: I've read that dogs should be taken out for a walk shortly after they have a meal. But I've also heard that if a dog is exercised right after eating, it could cause stomach bloat. I'm confused. *Should a dog be walked after eating or not?*

A: Your confusion is quite common. Eating tends to trigger the need to move the bowels for many dogs. Thus it is wise to walk them or let them out within a short time after they eat. The difficulty arises because of sloppy use of the word *exercise*. For many small dogs a walk around the block—in the course of which it does its business—is all the exercise required. But large dogs need much more physical activity to stay healthy and happy. That means a good run, or a greatly lengthened time spent walking over much longer distances. A number of large dogs, especially Great Danes, have a tendency to stomach bloat, or torsion. This can be a serious condition that in some cases even requires surgery. But a walk to give a large dog an opportunity to relieve itself is not the same thing as real exercise. The kind of strenuous exercise large dogs require can lead to stomach bloat, and should be carried out at other times of the day, but a mere walk will not cause problems.

74

Scraps About Scraps

Q: A bit of a tiff arose recently with some friends who say we are giving our Rottweiler far too many table scraps. He gets a great deal of exercise and is in no way overweight or unhealthy. *Is there any general rule about the amount or kind of table scraps a dog should be fed?*

A: Many dogs thrive on table scraps. The only danger is that you could throw off the nutritional balance of the dog's diet by giving the dog too much of one kind of food. But if it's a matter of some meat one time, some rice another, and some green beans (which many dogs love) still another time, there's no reason for concern. Let's remember that both humans and dogs survived quite nicely through untold millennia without anybody having a clue about nutrition—Vitamin C wasn't even discovered until 1911. Balance is the key, and that's a matter of common sense.

75

Peel Me a Grape?

Q: My small mixed-breed loves cottage cheese. I usually give her about half a cup with a little milk and a bit of leftover meat for her morning meal. In the evening she gets a seven-ounce can of dog food together with half a packet of semimoist food. I am told, however, that grown dogs shouldn't be fed as much in the way of dairy products. *Is it really a mistake to give an adult dog cottage cheese or other dairy products on a daily basis?*

A: Many adult dogs do not deal well with more than a modest intake of dairy products. In many dogs dairy products given in excess cause diarrhea. But if your dog's stools are firm and she likes cottage cheese, fine. Experts in dog nutrition can lay out general rules on what a dog should and should not be eating, but they are perfectly well aware that many dogs are highly individualistic in both what they like and their ability to flourish on somewhat offbeat diets. I once took care of a splendid Boxer for a couple of weeks while her owner was away. He instructed me that to keep

Tosca happy, I should give her a treat of iceberg lettuce sprinkled with Parmesan cheese every other day and that she was also extremely partial to seedless grapes fed to her by hand! And so it proved. She devoured the lettuce and drooled over the grapes. A craving for cottage cheese seems thoroughly conventional by contrast.

76

Pill Duplicities

Q: My Wirehaired Terrier, Biloxi, is like the heroine of some old black-and-white suspense movie when it comes to taking pills: She seems to suspect that somebody is out to poison her, and she has devised all kinds of stratagems to avoid ingesting them. I've been instructed by her veterinarian, as well as a helpful friend, in the art of putting them in Biloxi's mouth in a way that means she has to swallow them, but I just don't have the knack for it. She spits them out no matter what. Don't tell me to hide them in her food. She deposits them neatly alongside her bowl. *Is there anything wrong with putting a pill inside some kind of special snack like a piece of cheese in order to get a dog to swallow a pill?*

A: There are vets and dog owners who will look down their noses at you for doing this, making you feel like an incompetent bungler. Ignore them; they're like people who say, "You mean you really can't grow African violets?" A small piece of semisoft cheese is just fine. Some people swear by Fig Newtons, although here the sugar content is a little high. My own solution (I'm an incompetent in this regard myself) is to use about a third of a canned Vienna sausage. They're soft enough to insert a pill into with ease, and a dog has it swallowed before its suspicions are alerted.

Your Dog Isn't into Zen

Q: My younger sister is the sort of person who gets terribly caught up in causes, fads, and movements of all kinds. Recently she became a vegetarian, which is just fine; lots of people seem to lead very healthy lives on a diet that avoids meat. But now she has got it into her head that her dog should become a vegetarian too. *Is it possible for a dog to prosper on a vegetarian diet?*

A: Absolutely not! Dogs are carnivores, and their systems have evolved to depend on a high-protein diet that can be satisfied only by meat, poultry, fish and their by-products, plus eggs and dairy products. Dogs simply can't extract the necessary nutrients from vegetables and grains, and the attempt to do so will severely tax their entire system. What's more, even a dog that is fed meat can have problems if the diet also contains too much fiber, which blocks full absorption of many vitamins and minerals. Your sister might just as well try running her car on rubbing alcohol.

Beware of the Bone

Q: My Fox Terrier seems to have trouble dealing with bones. He chews on them until they splinter and then tends to throw pieces back up. *Is it a bad idea to give dogs bones to play with?*

A: Many veterinarians frown on giving dogs bones despite all the lore connected with the subject. Bones that are small enough to splinter easily can be dangerous; it is possible for a shard to actually puncture a dog's intestines. While some larger, harder bones can be okay for dogs that do play with the bone rather than trying to devour it, rawhide bones are really a better alternative.

79

More and Less

Q: With an eleven-year-old dog and a twelve-month-old puppy to feed simultaneously, we have changed the feeding times of the older dog. When they were on different schedules, with the puppy being fed four times a day and the older dog twice, the puppy was stealing the older dog's food. Now we feed them simultaneously three times a day. *Is it bad for an older dog to be fed three smaller meals a day?*

A: Quite the contrary. It is a schedule that many vets would recommend for an older dog anyway. Your puppy, of course, needs twice the amount of food an older dog does, in order to support its rapid growth. But things have to be kept in bounds, since too much food can lead to having an overweight dog or to growth so rapid that it can lead to other problems. By feeding the two simultaneously, you are avoiding the problem of the puppy getting too much food and at the same time the three smaller meals the older dog is getting are likely to be easier for it to digest.

One thing to remember about an older dog, however, is that while it may need fewer calories because it is more sedentary, it does still need plenty of protein. Some questions have been raised as to whether the special commercial foods targeted at older dogs contain sufficient protein. Other special-purpose dog foods, including those for puppies, pass muster with canine nutritionists across the board.

80

Chocolate Warnings

Q: Trying to be helpful, I seem to have caused a major problem with my sister-in-law, who lives only about an hour away. Visiting her one day, I saw her four-year-old daughter feeding M&Ms to their dog. I told my sister-in-law she should put a stop to it because chocolate was poisonous to dogs. I was informed I was being ridiculous and instructed to mind my own business. *Isn't it true that there is something in chocolate that is toxic to dogs?*

A: Yes, it's a substance called theobromine. It can cause very serious reactions in dogs, although some dogs are much more sensitive to it than others. Owners should also be careful about using cocoa-tree chips as a garden mulch; a dog that ingests these can become very sick indeed.

81

He Ate a Whole Bottle of Pills

Q: My dog recently devoured most of a bottle of pain-killing pills. I can't get the top off without a struggle and assumed it was safe to leave it on the bathroom-sink counter. He's in his "adolescence" and somehow took it into his mind to play with the bottle and then got it open and ingested its contents. Fortunately this occurred during the day, and I rushed him to the vet. But what if it had happened at night? *What is the best procedure to follow if a dog gets into something poisonous at night?*

A: First, check to see if there is a twenty-four-hour animal hospital in your neighborhood and have the address and telephone number handy. Know how to get there by car, so that no time will be wasted. Many smaller communities will not have an all-night facility, but if you have a good relationship with your vet and regularly bring your dog in for checkups and booster shots, he or she may be willing to give you a home number. Don't abuse that privilege, and your vet may be willing to respond to a poisoning emergency. There is also a twenty-four-hour National Animal Poison Control Center at the University of Illinois. The telephone number is 800–548–2423. There is a onetime twenty-five-dollar charge for the service (have your credit card handy). They will help as best they can. If you know what your dog has gotten into, have the bottle, cannister, or carton at hand; it should also be taken with you when you can get to a vet.

But the real focus here should be prevention. You may not have children, but think in terms of what you would keep locked up so that a two-year-old child couldn't get at it and follow the same routine with your dog. There are many things that can attract a dog, from sweet-smelling antifreeze to sugar-coated pills. Don't let it happen.

82

Chemicals on the Lawn

Q: I am about to embark on a second marriage to a wonderful man who is quite wealthy. He has a country house with expansive lawns that he pays a lot of money to keep in tiptop shape. Thus they are constantly being sprayed with all kinds of fertilizers, weed killers, and pest eradicators. I have a dog that although raised in the city is absolutely thrilled at being able to romp at will on these great green expanses. But I worry about all those chemicals. *Is there any danger to dogs from lawn-care products?*

A: The makers of lawn chemicals insist that their testing shows that there is no danger to pets once the chemicals have dried. This means keeping your pet off the lawn for a couple of hours after spraying. Subsequent rainstorms will *not* make the chemicals dangerous. You should, however, avoid spraying a lawn and using chemical flea sprays in the house simultaneously or even on the same day. Interactions between various kinds of chemical sprays are not fully understood, and caution is advised.

There are those, of course, who inveigh against the use of virtually all chemical sprays, which they believe are gradually polluting our planet beyond measure. They may be right, in the long run, but lawn-care products, properly handled, will not make your dog sick on the spot. Because dogs have relatively short life spans, it is more likely to be we humans who will bear the brunt of long-term adverse effects.

83

The Silent Bark

Q: I came home one day to find that my Schnauzer puppy had pulled over a dieffenbachia plant that was on a low bookcase next to a sofa. She came skulking in looking very wary as I stood over the plant. Since she really did seem to understand what she had done, I scolded her. She hung her head, but soon perked up. She had just recently discovered that she could bark, and she sat there with her jaw making barking motions. But nothing came out. Fortunately I had once read a short story about a woman who had put a little dieffenbachia leaf into a soup she then fed to her very loquacious husband, knowing that it temporarily paralyses the vocal chords when ingested. So I knew what had happened to my dog, and her bark returned a few hours later. But the incident set me to wondering. *Are there any houseplants that are actually poisonous to dogs?*

A: Yes, there are, including two Christmas favorites, the poinsettia and the amaryllis. The former inflames the mucous membranes as well as the lining of the esophagus and the stomach; the latter will cause vomiting very quickly.

Neither of these plants will cause very serious damage if you get the dog to drink lots of water or milk (unless your dog doesn't tolerate it well) so as to flush the system through urination.

While plants are less of a problem with dogs than cats, do keep them high enough off the ground to protect your puppy.

84

Heat Prostration

Q: I am about to move from Oregon to central Texas. My dog, a Poodle named Daisy, loves to ride around with me in the car. I am aware of the fact that you must leave windows at least partway open in hot weather so that a dog doesn't overheat while you go into a store, but I'm worried that in the much-hotter climate I'm moving to, even that may not be safe. *How dangerous is it to leave a dog in a car for twenty minutes or so during hot weather?*

A: It can be very dangerous, and I'm afraid Daisy is going to have to get used to staying at home more in the summer months. You are to be commended for your concern, however—it is astonishing how many dog owners refuse to take the matter of heat prostration in dogs seriously despite annual warnings by "Dear Abby," pet columns in newspapers, and local television-news programs. This is a case where ignorance or sheer disregard of warnings can lead all too easily to the death of a dog.

Dogs have a very inefficient cooling system. They cannot sweat through their skins the way we do, except at the very front of their paws. If they become very hot, the only way they can regulate their internal thermostats is by panting. And there is a point at which the panting itself becomes so fast that the exertion involved becomes a part of the problem. What's more, there must be currents of fresh air for panting to do much good for long. In a car with the windows closed, sitting in the sun, the temperature inside the vehicle can reach 115 degrees Fahrenheit in a matter of minutes; even with the windows lowered a couple of inches, the lack of air circulation is dangerous.

85

Shocking Behavior

Q: My Wirehaired Terrier puppy is fascinated by lamp cords and loves to chew on them. Some people have said that all it will take is one little shock to stop him, but I wonder. *Couldn't a puppy be seriously injured if it succeeded in biting through the outer coating of a lamp cord?*

A: Yes, it could. Take the precaution of taping loose cords to the baseboard to make them less tempting. This is one case where it is important to shout no, loudly enough to really startle your puppy, if you are lucky enough to catch him in the act. If you should find your puppy in apparent shock and having any trouble breathing, get him to the vet immediately. The danger here is not so much from any burn caused by the initial shock but from the fact that electrocution often leads to pulmonary edema, a buildup of fluid in the lungs that can be fatal.

If your dog still has the cord in his mouth, do not touch him without first disconnecting the cord, or you are liable to get a nasty shock yourself. You could also use a broom to move the dog away from the cord. In some cases it may be necessary to take preemptive action against a cord-chewing puppy by confining him in a room in which all cords are disconnected while you are out. But be sure to continue saying no every time the puppy goes near an electrical cord.

86

Getting an Injured Dog to the Vet

Q: When a human being falls and breaks a hip or is hit by a car, the rule is not to move the person until an ambulance arrives. But with a dog there is no ambulance to call, and you have to get the animal to the vet yourself. *What precautions can be taken to minimize further injury to an injured dog?*

A: This is a problem, because dogs that have been hit by cars in particular are likely to be suffering from internal bleeding. The best way to handle a small dog is to pick it up by the skin behind the neck. With a large dog you will need help to lift it onto a blanket, which should then be used as a kind of stretcher.

Dogs are very likely to go into shock when seriously injured, which will cause their temperatures to drop quickly. This can be at least as dangerous as any internal bleeding, so it is very important to keep the dog warm while it is being driven to the vet. And remember, don't speed. An automobile accident or even being stopped by a cop could doom your dog.

Hospital Visits

Q: My Doberman was recently hospitalized for several days following a poisoning incident. I was scolded by a couple of my dog-loving friends for not visiting her, but it was my feeling that if I showed up, she would think I was going to take her home and that it would only make her more despondent. *How do veterinarians generally feel about having the owner visit an ill dog?*

A: That depends on the character of the vet, the owner, and the dog. Even a vet who is generally in favor of such visits may discourage one from an owner who has a tendency to excessive second-guessing or potential hysteria. And some dogs appear to benefit from such a visit, while others feel doubly abandoned when the owner departs without the dog. Your approach is perfectly sensible. After all, you know your dog best, and it certainly isn't the business of anybody else. There are people who are born hospital visitors and will descend upon an ill person, dog, cat, or even bird, at the slightest opportunity. I am not sure their ministrations are always as appreciated as they seem to think.

88

Heartworm Warnings

Q: I'm a resident of Chicago, but I've been invited to spend a month this summer with my sister and her husband at their summer home in South Carolina. My dog will be going with me, and my sister says I should get a heartworm prescription from my veterinarian before I come. *How common is heartworm, and will drugs really protect my dog?*

A: Heartworm can be a problem in most areas, but it is an acute one in the Southeast. This is because of the prevalence of mosquitoes, which transmit the parasite from one dog to another. Heartworms, also called filariae, are an extremely dangerous parasite. They interfere with the flow of blood, cause difficulty in breathing—often accompanied by a cough—and sometimes lead to convulsions. In puppies and older dogs, heartworm is often fatal and is a dreadfully debilitating disease for any dog to suffer.

Although the larvae of the heartworm work their way quite slowly through the dog's system to the heart, by the

153

time they have reached a detectable stage, a dog will already be in trouble, and the parasite far more difficult to kill. Thus it is imperative that a dog have a daily dose of medicine, in either liquid or pill form, every day during mosquito season. The medicine kills the larvae just as they are transferred to the dog, at a point when they develop into a third stage in less than a day (the first two stages occur in the mosquito). Provided you see to it that your dog gets the preventative every twenty-four hours, it will be fully protected.

89

The Elusive Whipworm

Q: My dog had bloody diarrhea, so I took him to the vet. She said she "suspected" whipworms and gave Brownie medicine, which in fact worked. But I have wondered why she didn't run a variety of tests before prescribing a course of treatment. *Is it common to prescribe for whipworms on the basis of a "suspicion"?*

A: Yes, veterinarians often do this. The reason is that the presence of whipworms can be very difficult to detect; there may be no sign of their eggs in a dog's stool. An experienced vet's suspicions can be very accurate in a situation like this. Veterinarians fortunately have not reached the point, as have so many physicians, of running endless tests just to protect themselves against malpractice suits.

90

Flea Wars

Q: We moved to Florida two years ago from Minnesota. Up north we had a flea problem with our dogs in midsummer, but here the season seems to go on forever, and during it the battle is never-ending. We've tried every product on the market. *Isn't there any weapon against fleas that's really effective in driving out the marauding hordes?*

A: We American pet owners spend around a billion dollars a year on commercial antiflea arsenals, and all we manage to do is hold the line. In the South in general, and Florida in particular, it seems to most pet owners that they are in fact not even managing that. But then the entire planet is infested with the critters: There are at least 2,200 different species and subspecies, without even thinking about the number that may lurk, still unclassified, in the world's rain forests. The problem is that when it comes to multiplying, fleas make even the proverbial rabbit look like a piker.

Many experts think the problem is getting worse. One expert on the subject, James Blakemore of Purdue University, points an accusing finger at cats and shag carpets. Cats—because the chief tormenter in the United States is the cat flea, which prefers angora but will gladly settle for Sheepdogs. Since cats have now surpassed dogs in popularity as pets and are far less willing to sit still for a bath or a spray than dogs are, the problem has grown. Shag carpets, you ask? Perfect breeding grounds.

Is there any hope? Well, you've no doubt heard of the Twelve Step programs so popular in the human-potential movement. For eradicating fleas, experts have come up with a five-step program. First, you shampoo the cat or dog, then you spray it and slap a flea collar on it, all the while spraying the house and yard. Some people claim this does work, although they do admit that one side effect is becoming obsessed with jokes about how many people with pets it takes to screw in a lightbulb.

91

Natural Flea Controls?

Q: I have heard a good deal of talk lately about natural flea-control ingredients such as herbs and citrus oils. The chemical flea controls on the market really do worry me in terms not only of my dog's health but also that of my children. *Has anyone come up with real proof that natural flea controls work?*

A: The evidence is primarily anecdotal, largely because companies that have the research resources to test natural flea controls are the very ones that produce the chemical versions. The anecdotal reports are sometimes quite persuasive, but many of the herbs and plants used, such as pennyroyal and tansy, are difficult to come by unless you grow them yourself. The citrus oils and rinses could quite easily be produced at home, but they don't have the same reputation for effectiveness.

One alternative flea control that can be used to keep fleas from spawning in your carpet is 20 Mule Team Borax. Worked into the carpet with one's foot, this does seem to be quite helpful, but if your house is infested, you will still have to start with chemicals before turning to the borax as a continuing measure.

92

Lyme-Disease Facts

Q: We've just moved from Kansas City, Kansas, to western Massachusetts. Our new home is a wonderful Victorian house with nearly three acres of land, part of which has long grasses and a bushy, wooded area. I'm somewhat worried about our two dogs and our children, because I understand that this is a prime area for ticks that carry Lyme disease. *If the dogs were to get Lyme disease, could they pass it on to my children?*

A: No, the disease is not "communicable" in that sense and can be acquired only by being bitten by a tick that carries the disease. This is also true of the other most common tick-borne disease, Rocky Mountain spotted fever. There are three main sections of the country where ticks carrying these diseases are particularly common: from northern Massachusetts south to Maryland on the East Coast, in the Wisconsin-Minnesota area of the Midwest, and in northern California, Nevada, and Oregon.

Preventing your dogs and children (and yourselves) from getting Lyme disease or Rocky Mountain spotted fever is a matter of taking some simple precautions. During tick season, from May through August, it would be wise to keep the long grasses mown short and advise your children to stay out of tangled undergrowth. Your dogs can be sprayed with antitick solutions and may also be vaccinated against Lyme disease (inoculations for humans have not been approved as yet). But the best precaution of all is to go over your dogs and through your children's hair each evening. If you find any ticks, remove them with tweezers, as close as possible to the tip of the dug-in head, and dispose of them in a jar of rubbing alcohol, then clean the area with a cotton swab dipped in hydrogen-peroxide solution. Since it takes up to twelve hours for the tick to pass on the disease, a daily inspection should be sufficient if you keep your dogs on a leash for their last outing at night. If your children are seven years or older, you may be able to delegate the dogs' tick inspection to them. My sister and I were in charge of this detail for our Irish Setter when we were kids.

Fever and loss of appetite are early signs of both Lyme disease and Rocky Mountain spotted fever in dogs. A very distinct rash in the shape of a bull's-eye marks Lyme disease in humans, fever and more generalized rashes being signs of Rocky Mountain spotted fever. Both dogs and humans respond quickly to antibiotic treatment in the early stages. Take precautions and seek medical advice at any suspicious signs and you should have no real problems.

93

Mange Mites

Q: We live in a rather sparsely populated area where dogs are allowed to run at will. There is one dog roaming around that has mange. The dog has tags and disappears at night, so we assume it isn't a stray, but its condition worries us in terms of the health of our own dogs. *How communicable is mange?*

A: That depends on the kind of mange the dog has. One kind is highly contagious, the other hereditary and not usually contagious. The first kind is called sarcoptic mange, or scabies. It is caused by a mite that burrows into a dog's skin to lay its eggs, which then hatch and burrow back out again. The resulting raised areas of skin are terribly itchy, causing the dog to scratch endlessly. Treatment involves medicated shampoos and pesticidal dippings. These should be carried out by a veterinarian at least the first time around in case the dog has a bad reaction to the pesticide. A vet may also prescribe antibiotics to head off infections of wounds the dog has scratched open. The dog's bedding should also be treated as a precaution, but you don't have to worry about carpets, since the mite does not survive long without an animal host.

Demodectic mange is also caused by a mite, but this mite is often present on dogs without causing any problems. But some dogs—German Shepherds in particular—appear to have a hereditary inability to tolerate the mite, and it can proliferate out of control. Demodectic mange does not necessarily cause itching, but it does lead to hair loss and often to infections. While puppies sometimes get the mite from their mother, and it may cause problems because they are so vulnerable, this kind of mange is not considered contagious between adult dogs. Unfortunately treatment for demodectic mange is more difficult than for scabies, taking much longer and sometimes not succeeding.

94

Chronic Skin Problems

Q: Our next-door neighbors have a German Shepherd that seems to be constantly afflicted with skin problems. Its owners are nice people, but we can't help wondering if the dog is being properly cared for. *Could a dog that receives good care and is regularly taken to the vet have a chronic skin problem?*

A: Unfortunately yes. Many dogs are allergic to flea bites, for example. The resulting dermatitis can be severe. Not just skin irritation but also hair loss can easily result, and in some cases infections may also occur. But skin problems and hair loss can also be caused by physical problems that exist within the dog's own system, such as endocrine gland malfunction. In general there are so many varieties of skin problems that can afflict dogs that it can be a constant battle to keep ahead of them. There are chronic cases in which both veterinarian and owner come to the conclusion that it is kinder to have a dog put to sleep than to let it suffer any longer. Never jump to the conclusion that an otherwise well-cared-for dog with serious skin problems is not being given the medical attention it needs. Some owners have spent small fortunes trying to cure skin problems to no avail.

95

Floppy-Ear Care

Q: Dogs with big, floppy ears have always seemed especially appealing to me. But as I consider what kind of dog to get now that I am off on my own (my mother is an interior decorator and was firmly a no-pet lady), I am told by a friend that floppy ears are prone to medical problems. This seems strange to me—wouldn't they protect the inner ear? *What kind of medical problems are likely to arise with floppy-eared dogs?*

A: Because large, floppy ears cut off air circulation, they can create an environment in which bacteria flourish within the ear, leading to infection. Some breeds tend to grow a good deal of hair on the underside of the ear, which can shed and form ear plugs that also foster harmful bacterial growth. This is no reason to avoid floppy-eared dogs; it just means that the owner must pay some extra attention to ear hygiene.

Another medical problem that can develop with floppy-eared dogs is tearing of the lower edges of the ear. This is less likely to occur with house pets, but can be a problem with hunting dogs that are used in rough country with a lot of underbrush. Such ear tears may require surgery to repair.

96

What Terrible Breath You Have, My Dear

Q: My six-year-old dog's breath has been very bad lately. *Is bad breath in a dog a sign of tooth decay?*

A: Dogs don't usually develop cavities, although it can occur when an overly indulgent owner feeds a dog candies on a regular basis. Tartar is another matter; it builds up on a dog's teeth just as it does on ours. Rawhide chews can help to combat tartar, but if it does get out of hand, your veterinarian can scale it away.

You should be aware, however, that bad breath can be a sign of more serious problems, ranging from digestive problems to some kind of mouth infection. A dog with chronic bad breath should be taken in for a thorough checkup.

97

How Dare You Sneeze on My Pekingese!

Q: I recently took care of a friend's Pekingese for a week while she went off to visit her family for Thanksgiving. I had a bad cold when my friend came to pick up her beloved Trisket, and instead of sympathizing with me she practically snapped, "I certainly hope you didn't give your cold to Trisket!" I was really quite annoyed. *Can a dog really catch a cold from a human being?*

A: Pekingese have a history as royal lapdogs stretching back to ancient China, and Trisket obviously has an owner willing to put her before anything, including manners. Your friend should know better. Dogs certainly cannot get a cold from a human being. Nor can a human being get a cold from a dog. The viruses that do afflict both humans and dogs cannot be transmitted between the two species, although similar symptoms may be evident.

98

A Sunburned Nose

Q: My Collie has developed some scabs on the end of its nose. My longtime veterinarian retired, and I'm dealing with a new, young one who says that the trouble with my Collie is sunburn! *Is it really true that a dog's nose can become sunburned?*

A: Your new vet may be young, but it sounds as though he or she is right on target. Collies are particularly vulnerable to sunburn at the tip of the nose because of the very light pigmentation there. The scabs appear because the dog is scratching the affected area, so the chief danger is infection. Antibiotics can take care of the infection, and sunblock can prevent the condition from reappearing.

99

Water Dogs

Q: We have just bought a house with a considerable lake-front expanse. And after years of city living, we have promised our three children, ages five to twelve, that they can have a dog. The whole family agrees that it would be nice to have a dog that likes to swim and play in the water. *What breeds of dog are particularly happy about swimming?*

A: The Retriever breeds, including the Labrador, Curly-Coated, and Chesapeake Bay varieties, are all waterfowl-hunting dogs and love the water. So do Irish and English Setters. More unusual possibilities include the Italian Spinone, a large white or white-with-orange dog with a very thick coat, and the Wirehaired Pointing Griffon, which also has a thick coat, usually gray with brown patches or all brown, and which prefers to live outdoors. But perhaps the ultimate water dog is the Newfoundland, which has a strong instinct as a rescue dog and has been used around the world for that purpose. As noted earlier, it is also wonderful with children—although any of these water-loving dogs is a fine choice in that regard.

100

Frisbee Dogs

Q: My dog is a mutt if there ever was one, but she does have a remarkable talent for playing Frisbee. I've been told that there are serious competitions for such dogs. *Are there organized events for "Frisbee dogs," or are these just country-fair types of things that pop up in local communities?*

A: There is a national championship each year: The 1992 finals were held in Washington, D.C., following a half-dozen regional championships across the country. One of the nice things about this championship is that the ancestry of the dogs doesn't count for anything. Showmanship, leaping ability, and the degree of difficulty of the catches are the criteria, making it possible for the most thorough-going mongrel to achieve great acclaim and even make it to the evening news.

101

Firehouse Dog

Q: In our town there is a splendid Dalmatian that rides with the fire truck, a sight that enchants my young son. I gather that it is quite common for this breed to be a firehouse mascot. *How did the tradition of Dalmatians riding fire trucks get started?*

A: The association between Dalmatians and firehouses goes back centuries. Particularly in England, the Dalmatian was very popular as a stable dog, a coach dog, trotting alongside horsedrawn carriages, and—since fire engines were also horsedrawn—as a firehouse dog. Due to its considerable abilities as a rat catcher, it was a very useful animal to have around stables. A fearless dog with an ability to stay put in one place when told to, it is perfectly happy riding high on a speeding fire truck.

102

Racing for Its Life

Q: In our locality there is a flourishing dog track that races Greyhounds. I have mixed feelings about the whole endeavor (although other people will say, "What's the difference between racing dogs and horses?"). But I understand that many Greyhounds are destroyed once their racing days are over. *If one adopted a racing Greyhound after its running days, would it make a suitable pet?*

A: Let's start with a little history here—ancient history, since Greyhounds have existed for at least five thousand years. Carvings on Egyptian and Assyrian tombs and monuments make clear that the breed has changed very little down through the millennia, less than any other breed. It is the fastest of all dogs, and its natural quarry is the hare—which is why mechanical "rabbits" are used in Greyhound racing. This practice began in England in the 1870s, but became particularly prevalent in the United States. Today there are tracks throughout the world, from Europe to Australia

Animal-rights activists have targeted Greyhound racing as inhumane, but they are countered by a growing number of animal experts who feel that many breeds of dog are in fact far happier performing the hunting or working tasks they were originally bred for than as cossetted pets—and Greyhounds were bred for racing. The sport is highly regulated, but there are sometimes problems with abuse. Most disturbingly to many people, a lot of Greyhounds, about 50 percent, are put to sleep after their racing abilities begin to wane at about three and a half years of age. A program coordinated by the American Greyhound Council, however, is dedicated to finding homes for "retired" racers, placing about seven thousand dogs a year. They make quiet and affectionate house pets. It is important to see to it that they continue to get a lot of exercise. Greyhounds are not, however, the best bet for a family with very young children, since they do not like to be teased.

103

A Companion for the Handicapped

Q: An automobile accident has left our twelve-year-old daughter in a wheelchair. She has full use of her upper body, but only limited use of her legs, although we hope that will improve with continued therapy. A number of people have suggested, and we ourselves feel, that a dog would be very helpful to Susan as a companion in the difficult teenage years to come. *What breeds of dog are particularly good with handicapped people?*

A: It is now widely accepted that dogs (and cats) can offer important emotional support to handicapped people, and you are wise to be considering such a companion for your daughter. While there are many breeds of dog that could serve the purpose well, none can match the Shetland Sheepdog. Shelties, as they are often called, are unwaveringly loyal, affectionate, and gentle. They are also highly intelligent and possess an exceptional sensitivity to human moods, to which they readily adapt. Some people regard them as almost "telepathic."

Smaller than a Collie but similar in coloring and shape, these wonderful herding dogs from the Shetland Islands do need a good deal of grooming to keep their long coats in good condition, but since your daughter has full use of her upper body, the grooming task should prove no problem for her and can only increase her bond with the dog.

104

Seeing Eyes

Q: I am curious about the term "Seeing Eye dog." *Is the reason so many German Shepherds are used as Seeing Eye dogs that they have particularly good eyesight?*

A: All of a German Shepherd's senses are highly developed, with the sense of smell preeminent, as is true with all dogs. What makes the German Shepherd a superb Seeing Eye dog for the blind is its great intelligence and remarkable trainability. The German Shepherd, in fact, is probably the most versatile of all dogs in terms of the number of specialized tasks it is capable of doing well. From sniffing out drugs to searching for survivors in the rubble of buildings brought down by earthquakes, as a guard dog or lifesaver, the potential usefulness of the German Shepherd is difficult to top. They are also exceptionally loyal to an owner and they're masters at keeping people out of harm's way. While there are several other breeds that make good Seeing Eye dogs, the German Shepherd is unsurpassed at the job.

105

My Dog the Rat Catcher

Q: A college classmate of mine and her husband recently bought an old farm out in the country. In one of her letters my friend said that they were delighted their dog has turned out to be such an expert rat and mouse catcher. I am a cat person myself, and perhaps I'm just feeling that a major cat talent is being made light of here, but I find it difficult to believe my friend's story and suspect I am being teased. *Are some dogs actually good at catching mice and rats?*

A: Most certainly. Several of the Terrier breeds, most particularly the Yorkshire, the Manchester, and the Dandie Dinmont, were bred to be ratters and given the job of keeping farmyards, warehouses, and the mines of northern England free of rodents. They were felt to be better at the job than cats, because they were more aggressive and because their ratting instincts were not connected with the eating of the rodent. They simply killed them. It should be said, however, that while most cats are good at catching mice and rats, only a few specific breeds of dog are.

106

Fits of Jealousy

Q: After my divorce five years ago I acquired a wonderful little Shih Tzu that has been a dear companion. I am now deeply involved with a man I am going to marry shortly, who spends much time at my apartment, since it is far closer to where we both work than his is. My husband-to-be loves dogs, but my Mandy is not only extremely standoffish but has also started soiling the floor on occasion and even tearing up shoes like a puppy. *What can be done with a dog that is resisting the presence of a new person in one's life?*

A: Your dog is furiously jealous. The breed has a tendency to be distant with strangers, but in your case this characteristic has been compounded by rage that she is not getting your undivided attention. This is the downside of the great loyalty of the breed. I wish I could suggest that your Mandy will settle down with time, but you may have continuing problems that will make it necessary to go back to training basics and do it very firmly. It may even be necessary to seek the help of a private trainer who specializes in "dog psychology."

107

Dachshund Doings

Q: My daughter has taken it into her head that the dog she had been promised for her seventh birthday must be a Dachshund. I can certainly understand the attraction, since they seem to be such lively and amusing creatures, but I am somewhat wary because I have heard about a lot of people whose Dachshunds have had a variety of physical problems. *Are Dachshunds more prone to health problems than average?*

A: The chief physical problem that affects Dachshunds is slipped disks in the spinal cord. This can cause paralysis. The incidence is not high enough to deter Dachshund lovers, but the possibility always exists. The females of the breed can also develop false pregnancies, and mammary tumors are fairly common.

Despite such potential problems, Dachshunds have long been greatly favored as pets. The Shorthaired, or Smooth, Dachshund is particularly in demand because it does not shed, but there are also wirehaired and longhaired strains that are officially recognized. A badger-hunting dog of great courage and individuality, Dachshunds do need a firm hand in terms of training, since they can be quite stubborn and delight in outsmarting the owner. A Dachshund may know full well, for instance, that it is not allowed on the furniture, but it will never give up trying to sneak a nap on the sofa. But for many owners it is this very mischievousness that makes the breed so endearing.

108

Guard Dog, Watch Dog, Pet

Q: Having bought a house in a somewhat isolated area, we feel that we should have a guard dog. On the other hand, we don't want a dog that has to be kept chained up a lot of the time, but rather one that can also be a family pet. *What breeds might make good guard dogs as well as good pets?*

A: Like many people, you are failing to make a distinction between a guard dog and a watch dog. Guard dogs are trained not just to warn of intruders but to attack them. They must be trained by professionals, and while in some cases they may have an off-duty home with a trainer, it is seldom in a family situation. When it comes to watch dogs, however, which will warn you of anything out of place and at the same time make any intruder think several times about proceeding further, you have a wide choice of breeds that will also make excellent pets. A good watch dog does not even have to be a large dog. In fact some of the best are small, such as the Dachshund, which has a bark that sounds as though it is emanating from a dog several times its size, and even the tiny Lhasa Apso, whose Tibetan nickname was Barking Lion Sentinel Dog.

Guard dogs are for military and industrial complexes, warehouses, and the occasional estate owned by a potential James Bond villain. What you want is a good watch dog, and there are a great many possible choices.

109

Fear of Dogs

Q: I have a cousin who lives only fifty miles away and thus comes to visit every six weeks or so. Every time she does, I have to put my Miniature Schnauzer, Mitzi, in the back bedroom and close the door, because my cousin is terrified of dogs. Mitzi is not happy, and I am becoming increasingly irritated myself. *Can someone really be so frightened of a Miniature Schnauzer, or is a considerable degree of self-indulgence involved in such "fears"?*

A: I can understand your annoyance. A man once came to my house to discuss the possibility of my writing a book with him. My extremely sweet and gentle Border Collie mix went over to the sofa he was sitting on and put a paw on his knee to say hello. He was practically sitting on the sofa arm in seconds trying to get away from her. I could hardly keep a straight face—the man was a child psychologist! (No, I did not work with him.)

However, there is no question that some people are indeed terrified of dogs, no matter how small or how gentle.

To make matters worse, I think dogs sense the fear and try extra hard to snuggle up and make friends, which simply makes the dog hater feel as though he is being pursued by the Hound of the Baskervilles. Obviously a fear of this kind, one that has nothing to do with the dog at hand or present circumstances, involves some childhood incident that has never been properly dealt with. If a person really wants to get over this phobia, it can be done, but it requires that the phobic agree to spend at least a few minutes at a time getting to know a particular dog, with repeated encounters over a period of time, each one lasting a little longer. It depends on your relationship with your cousin whether you want to insist that such an approach at least be tried.

110

Legal Beagles

Q: We have four dogs. To be nearer to my husband's elderly parents, we are considering a move to another state. *As owners of several dogs, do we need to worry about restrictive laws in another part of the country?*

A: You most certainly do. Across the country more laws are being passed every year concerning dog ownership, and some of them are very restrictive. In terms of your own situation, there are a growing number of communities that restrict the number of dogs people can own, often limiting the number to two or at most three. But the legal situation in regard to dogs goes far beyond limitations on numbers. Licensing enforcement is becoming tougher, with animal-control officers going door-to-door in many localities demanding to be shown current license certificates as well as rabies-shot confirmation by a veterinarian. Some communities, such as San Mateo, California, have passed ordinances that owners either get breeding licenses or have their dogs neutered. Finally, definitions of what constitutes a "dangerous" dog are getting extremely broad in some localities, to the extent that a dog that merely barks at the man reading the water meter could be officially cited, and there are movements to outlaw particular breeds such as the Pit Bull.

For dog owners the proliferation of dog-related laws makes it essential to check out ahead of time the laws in force in any community they might be considering moving to. Pamphlets that list the current laws are usually available from the animal-control departments, humane shelters, or city hall in a given town or city. Write ahead and get the full story before you make a final decision about moving to a particular locale.

111

Pit-Bull Politics

Q: Our new neighbors in this semirural area have a Pit Bull. The dog is kept in a large fenced area, but it still makes us nervous. *Aren't Pit Bulls extremely vicious and dangerous dogs?*

A: Pit Bulls are without a doubt the most controversial dog breed there is at present. There are many who believe that Pit Bulls are inherently dangerous and ought to be eradicated as a breed. The British Parliament has passed laws to bring about that very end in England. What the English pointedly call an American Pit Bull, as well as three other little-known breeds, cannot be bred in England and are destroyed if owners don't have them neutered. In this country there are drives to enact similar laws in many localities.

But the breed also has its very vocal defenders, who say that there is nothing wrong with the breed, only with some owners, who are themselves vicious types who don't understand dogs and bought a Pit Bull as a kind of "macho" statement. In other words, it's the old nature-versus-nurture argument in a new area. Yes, the breed's defenders say, Pit Bulls were bred as dogfight contestants, but they, like the now-beloved Bulldog, are noble creatures at heart that have in the past been misused by human beings. Defenders also claim that the media has gone off the deep end about Pit Bulls, developing a thesis comparable to the 1950s McCarthy smear that if you were a member of the State Department, you were probably a "Commie." This controversy isn't going to end anytime soon, and there is evidence on both sides that can seem utterly convincing at any given moment. To be fair, I'd say any nervousness you may feel about having a Pit Bull in the neighborhood should take into account what you think about the character of the dog's owners as much as any "vicious dog" label.

112

If Your Dog Bites Someone

Q: I get the impression from newspaper stories that if my dog ever bit anyone, he would be considered guilty until proven innocent, no matter how much he had been provoked. *Have all the stories in recent years about dangerous dogs made it impossible for a dog to get a fair shake in a situation where the dog was clearly not at fault?*

A: Impossible, no, but this is an increasingly difficult situation in terms of justifying the dog's behavior. There is a lot of hysteria out there about dangerous dogs, and many new laws have stacked the deck against the dog—which has never had it easy in this context. Add on the mania for suing people that exists in this country and you can have a great deal of difficulty with police, animal-control officers, and, above all, the courts. If you can't produce a current certificate to show that the dog has been vaccinated against rabies, you are going to be in terrible trouble. Your dog will at the very least be impounded for a minimum ten-day observation period, and if any doubt exists, your dog will be put to sleep, since the presence of rabies can only be fully determined by analysis of the dog's brain.

Take a look at the comic strips: These days the only animal attacking the mailman is a cat named Garfield. There's a reason for this, in terms of societal attitudes, and every dog owner must take stringent precautions to keep his or her dog out of situations where the dog can be provoked. Those with guard dogs should take note that even the posting of warning signs won't necessarily afford much legal protection. These days it is necessary to police the police dogs. Take extra care.

113

Travel Accommodations

Q: Our family has decided to do something different this summer, since the children are now old enough to travel well. We're going to tour through a number of eastern states visiting Civil War battlefields. We want to take our dog, a Terrier mix, with us, but wonder if having a dog along is going to create difficulties in finding accommodations. *Are there a sufficient number of motels that allow pets to make an extended car trip with our dog advisable?*

A: There are plenty of motels, and even hotels, that do accept dogs, but there are a lot more that don't. There can be many reasons why a motel won't accept pets, running the gamut from the reasonable to the eccentric. In some localities there may be an ordinance against accommodating travelers with pets—the county health department, for example, may disallow pets in any rooms or cabins that have cooking facilities, even if it's only a hot plate. There are motels that will allow pets but tell you that the dog cannot be left alone in the room. There are motel owners that make the absence of pets a sales point: I have seen signs proclaiming, "No Pets Allowed. A Safe Haven for Allergy Sufferers." And of course some people just don't like or are afraid of dogs, and don't want them around.

All of this makes it extremely unwise to start off on a trip with a dog in an improvisatory way ("Let's see how far we get for today and then look for a place"). If you do that, you may find yourself driving around for hours desperately searching for a sign that says, "Pets Welcome." Plan ahead, and make reservations when traveling with a dog. Most major travel guides include information about which motels and hotels will accept pets, and there are also several books that focus entirely on this issue, the little classic in this field being the Quaker Oats Company's *Touring with Towser,* which is available for three dollars from Quaker Professional Services, 585 Hawthorne Center, Galesberg, Illinois 61401.

114

Time Passing

Q: I work nine to five, and although my Maltese does not make a fuss when I leave, does nothing destructive while I am out, and greets me with great affection, I still some-times feel a twinge of guilt about how much time she must spend by herself. *Do dogs have a real sense of the passing of time?*

A: There is a good deal of debate on this subject. They do not, obviously, have any numerical sense of time in the sense that human beings have. There are some experts who contend that there is really no way of knowing to what extent a dog can grasp the passing of blocks of time. But others feel that it can be deduced from certain behaviors that dogs do know, for instance, when it is time for an owner to come home.

As to whether dogs in general are less happy with single owners who are away from home for a prescribed period five or six days to work, it is very difficult to say. Some dogs make clear that they are unhappy, by barking, urinating, or destructive tearing up of the house. But it is perfectly possible to train a dog to stop doing these things. A well-trained dog, as your Maltese clearly is, is accepting of its owner's "lifestyle." For that dog, that is simply the way things are. So long as the dog gets lots of attention and affection when the owner is home, it is probably thoroughly content with its life. Remember that dogs sleep a lot more than we do. Some owners who have owned a number of dogs at various points in their lives under somewhat different living circumstances feel that dogs that are left alone during a working day adjust by sleeping more during the day and less than other dogs when the owner is home at night.

It should be added, however, that there are some breeds of dog that do not like to be left alone at all. This is particularly true of many of the toy dogs and of the Lhasa Apso. Quite a lot of people make the wrong assumption that because they are small, toy dogs are somehow like cats and thus need less attention. This could not be farther from the truth.

115

Home Care Versus Kennel Care

Q: When my wife and I go away, we ask a friend to feed our Beagle. He has a "home" in the garage, with a swinging door that opens onto a fenced yard. Our friend comes by twice a day to do the feeding and to play for a bit. Some people feel that this is somehow bad for the dog and that it would be happier in a kennel, where there are at least other dogs and people coming and going much more of the time. *Aren't most dogs really happier if they can stay at home when the owner is away?*

A: Of course. Some owners manage to persuade themselves that kennels are some kind of resort hotel with organized game programs and lots of company. There are some kennels that do take extra steps to keep their boarders happy, but they are very expensive. A situation such as your own, however, certainly is going to be less traumatic for the dog than even the best kennel. Your dog is on his own territory, can move about as he pleases, and gets to visit with your friend, with whom he already has a relationship, twice a day.

When a dog is confined to an apartment, the choice becomes a little more difficult, but depending on the individual dog, being at home can still be preferable. I do think it is important, however, that at least two people be involved in caring for the dog. If you can arrange for a second person to drop by once a day, it will be even better for the dog and provides backup. People do get into automobile accidents and have heart attacks, and if anything should happen to the one friend caring for your dog, the consequences could be tragic for your pet as well.

116

Dogs Like Presents Too

Q: I was Christmas shopping with a friend who surprised me by asking if I'd bought anything to wrap for our family dog (our first), who will be nine months old this December. Homer (yes, I'm afraid our name is Simpson) has quite a lot of toys, and there's always a box of treats in the house. *Do dogs really get any special pleasure out of having a wrapped present under the tree?*

A: And how! I once had a Border Collie–Terrier mix that received her first Christmas present when she was about eight months old. It was a rubber squeak toy of Disney's Pluto dressed in a Santa Claus suit. The toy was wrapped up and left under the tree before we went out to a party on Christmas Eve. When we got home, we found torn wrapping paper under the tree. Little Louise was nowhere in sight, but suddenly came bounding in with her new toy in her mouth, dropped it at our feet, and sat back and looked up at us. She had not touched another present, only her own, presumably having identified it by its "squeak-toy smell." Louise was (excuse me) an exceptionally bright creature, but I have heard similar stories.

Remember that dogs crave affection and closeness to the family. Including them in the festivities on Christmas morning will give them a real charge, and watching them unwrap their two or three treasures can be a delight for all. It is wise to keep the dog's presents on a high shelf in a closet until the ceremony begins, however, to guard against early unwrapping.

117

The Arthritic Dog

Q: Our last dog, a beautiful Irish Setter named Tara, developed serious arthritis when she was about eleven, and we had to have her put to sleep less than two years later—she couldn't even get up the three front steps to the house. We hated seeing her suffer so much. Now we're thinking of getting another dog. *Are there any breeds of dog that are less likely to suffer from arthritis?*

A: While there is some evidence that Irish Setters may be slightly more prone to arthritis than most breeds, it is in no way a breed characteristic. Nor can any breed be touted as sufficiently less likely to get arthritis to make that an issue in choosing a dog. It should be understood that there are several different kinds of arthritis. Degenerative and rheumatoid arthritis occur in numerous older dogs, although the former is a matter of eroding cartilage due to ordinary physical stress over a lifetime, and the latter is a disease that causes swelling in the joints. Aspirin is used to reduce pain in both conditions, just as it is for humans.

Infectious bacterial arthritis, however, can occur at any age, usually as the result of puncture injuries, including dog bites. Treatment for this condition is considerably more complicated and may require surgery. But again, the breed of dog involved is essentially irrelevant.

118

A Clouded Eye

Q: My Cocker Spaniel's eyes have become slightly opaque in the last couple of years. She's almost ten, and my vet says this haziness of the lens of the eye is perfectly normal and nothing to worry about. But my mother had cataracts, and I can't help wondering if this isn't something similar. *Do the eyes of all dogs get a little hazy with age?*

A: Yes. Cataracts are an abnormal growth that must be removed to prevent blindness. All dogs add thin layers of material to the lens as they age. The process is known as lenticular, or nuclear, sclerosis, which sounds ominous, but it is indeed completely normal and will not affect your dog's sight.

119

Blind to Blindness

Q: We live in a house with a fenced yard, which makes it possible for our dog to play on his own. Recently we took Rick with us when we went to visit some friends for the weekend. Rick had been there before, although not for several months, and he seemed very disoriented, bumping into furniture and stumbling on some steps. I took him to the vet the following day and was told that Rick was blind and could have been for some time. I was so shocked, I didn't ask some questions I should have. *How is it possible not even to notice that your dog has lost his sight?*

A: Many dogs adapt to blindness so well, by using their other senses, that they can function in their accustomed environment with an ease that is astonishing. It is not uncommon for an owner to fail to recognize that anything is wrong.

120

Three Legs and Thriving

Q: Our son, who lives a thousand miles away, has a dog that was recently badly injured when he was hit by a car. One of the dog's rear legs had to be amputated. We know how much the dog means to our son, but wonder if it wouldn't have been a kindness to the animal to have put it to sleep, even though he says it is doing fine. *How much do dogs with an amputated limb suffer, and how well do they manage on three legs?*

A: Many dogs fare amazingly well on three legs, although it is more difficult if the missing limb is a foreleg. Very large or obese dogs, however, may have a serious problem. Once the wound is healed, a dog should not suffer any pain. Some owners have even saved dogs that have lost two rear legs, by building a harness and wheeled chariot for the hindquarters. With the benefit of such a "wheelchair," it can be possible for a dog to race around at considerable speed. Only a rather special dog and owner can cope with such an arrangement, however. The owner may well have to fend off busybody charges of animal abuse, which can also crop up in the case of a three-legged dog. The operative question is very simple: Is the dog happy?

121

An Old-Age Companion?

Q: Our Poodle is twelve years old now and slowing down a good deal, although he is in generally good health. We were thinking of getting a puppy to keep him company and, not incidentally, to help cushion the eventual loss of Bongo, who is beloved by our children. *Will an old dog take well to the presence of a new puppy?*

A: Unlike old cats, which tend to be jealous and set in their ways, many old dogs take very well to having a puppy around. I have seen many old dogs perk up a lot in reaction to a new addition to the family. What's more, the "grandpa," as it were, will help to socialize and even train your new puppy.

There are some caveats here, though. Most toy dogs will not be at all happy to have competition for an owner's affection. There are also a number of breeds that tend to be "one-man dogs," such as Cairn Terriers and Lhasa Apsos, which will not like the situation at all. And of course it is important that the old dog be in general good health, as yours is.

122

He's in My Will

Q: As a widow in my late sixties with heart trouble, I am concerned about what would happen to my five-year-old Miniature Schnauzer, Albert, if I should die. *Is it regarded as eccentric to make provisions for a dog in one's will?*

A: All sorts of perfectly sensible things are regarded as eccentric by opinionated busybodies, but don't let that stop you. There is always the occasional nut case who leaves a vast estate to a pet, while cutting off all relatives without a dime, but a great many people make reasonable provisions for pets in their wills, and wisely.

It is imperative to find a relative, friend, or neighbor who will agree in advance to take charge of your dog. Try to find a backup person as well, in case circumstances change. If you find someone who is willing to give your pet a home and pay for its care out of his or her own pocket, you will be fortunate indeed. But you should certainly at least offer to leave a certain amount of money to offset the expenses of keeping the pet well fed and healthy. The amount decided upon can either be made as a direct payment to the new caregiver or be set up as a trust to be disbursed over time.

If you are unable to find anyone to take your dog, contact local rescue organizations. Some are better than others, so the possibilities should be thoroughly checked out. With proper funding provided, many such organizations will agree to keep your dog until a good home is found for it.

Whatever provisions you make, be sure that your attorney writes them up in language as scrupulous as is used in any other clause in your will. The courts consider pets to be property, just like your car or diamond ring, and the same kind of language must be used in respect to an animal.

123

Wonder(ful) Dogs

Q: Stories regularly appear in newspapers about dogs that have warned their owners about a fire or rescued a small child from drowning. Clearly most of these stories are true. *But how common is it for dogs to perform "heroic" acts and are certain breeds more likely to do so?*

A: Some dogs, from Newfoundlands to Chesapeake Bay Retrievers, have extremely strong "rescue" instincts. But dogs of every breed have been known to do extraordinary things in emergencies, seeming to surpass their own capabilities. A dog that has been trained, even just as a game, to "go get" can amaze by getting something it has never been really introduced to, such as a telephone receiver for an owner who has fallen and broken a hip. But even dogs with no special obedience training can indeed sense danger and issue warnings, or simply bark nonstop until someone comes to see what is wrong.

The underlying fact here is that most dogs are far more sensitive to human moods and emotions than we give them credit for. I once moved into the apartment of friends to take care of their Basset Hound, named Bip (after one of the characters created by the great mime Marcel Marceau). I came down with a very severe flu. Generally Bip was hard to control on a leash; he was always pulling ahead. But once he understood that I was ill, he pulled not at all and tolerated a very short walk. What's more, he went to the basket he slept in, pulled out the blanket in it with his teeth, dragged it to the side of my bed, and slept there for the three-day duration of my illness. I got up only to walk him briefly and feed him. That was nearly thirty years ago, but it leaves me deeply touched to this day.

124

Another Dog Too Soon?

Q: A neighbor in the large apartment building I live in lost her dog to old age recently. As it happened, my daughter had a Cocker Spaniel that had just had a litter and was looking for good homes for the dogs. I offered my neighbor one of the puppies, completely gratis, but she very curtly refused. I was quite taken aback by her manner. *Isn't the best way to deal with the death of a dog to get a new one right away?*

A: Many people do find that acquiring a new dog is the most salutary way to deal with such a loss. With young children it may be very important to take this course, although in such a situation it is doubly important to make sure that the new dog comes from a very reputable source. For a child to lose a beloved dog and then have the replacement puppy die in a few weeks can be devastating.

But there are also numerous people who can't bear the thought of getting a new dog for some time. They need to go through a grieving process that is akin to that following the loss of an important person in their lives. It is not at all uncommon for a grieving dog owner to react to odd little noises with the thought, "Oh, that must be Spot." This can happen for months on a gradually decreasing basis. At length Spot will come to be accepted as part of the past, and the dog lover will be ready for a new pet. Your gesture was certainly good-hearted and generous, but don't hold your neighbor's response too much against her.

125

A Memorial to a Dog

Q: When I go to church these days, I am getting quite a lot of dirty looks. The reason for this is that word has gotten out—although I told very few people and none from my church—that I had my dog buried in a dog cemetery. Apparently quite a number of my fellow church members think this is sacrilegious. I'm nearly eighty, and my husband died twenty years ago. I visit his grave every week, and I plan to do the same with the grave of my splendid Pomeranian, Vicky, who gave me fourteen years of utter devotion and intense delight. *Is there anything one can say to people to make them understand that a dog can, under certain circumstances, be the most important creature in one's life?*

A: I'm not sure how much good it will do—prejudice is prejudice—but you could tell them about Lord Byron and his Newfoundland named Boatswain. When Boatswain died, Byron caused a considerable scandal by having him buried in the ruins of the great abbey at Newstead. There were those who were even more scandalized by the words he had inscribed on the headstone, celebrating his companion as possessing "all the Virtues of Man without his vices."

There are millions who understand that sentiment completely.

Bibliography

Ammer, Christine. *It's Raining Cats and Dogs*. New York: Paragon, 1989.

Bauman, Diane. *Beyond Basic Dog Training*. New York: Howell Book House, 1991.

Benjamin, Carol Lea. *Mother Knows Best*. New York: Howell Book House, 1985.

————. *Second Hand Dog*. New York: Howell Book House, 1988.

Burnham, Patricia Gail. *Playtraining Your Dog*. New York: St. Martin's Press, 1985.

Bygrave, Lesley, and Paul Dodd. *Practical Training for Big Dogs*. New York: Howell Book House, 1989.

Caras, Roger (Ed.). *Harper's Illustrated Handbook of Dogs*. New York: HarperCollins, 1985.

Carson, Delbert, and James Griffin. *The Dog Owner's Home Veterinary Handbook*. New York: Howell Book House, 1980.

Cole, William (Ed.). *Man's Funniest Friend*. Cleveland: World, 1967.

————*The Complete Dog Book*. New York: Howell Book House, 1985.

Dibra, Bashkim, with Elizabeth Randolph. *Dog Training by Bash*. New York: Signet, 1992.

Evans, Job Michael. *The Evans Guide for Counseling Dog Owners.* New York: Howell Book House, 1985.

Fox, Michael J. *Understanding Your Dog.* New York: Coward, 1972.

Harper, Joan. *The Healthy Cat and Dog Cook Book.* New York: Dutton, 1979.

Hearne, Vicki. *Adam's Task.* New York, Vintage, 1987.

Johnson, Norman H., with Saul Galin. *The Complete Puppy and Dog Book.* New York: Atheneum, 1968.

Kay, William J., with Elizabeth Randolph. *The Complete Book of Dog Health.* New York: Howell Book House, 1985.

Kohl, Sam. *All About Dog Shows.* Neptune, N.J.: TFH Publications, 1986.

Lytton, Hon. Mrs. Neville. *Toy Dogs and Their Ancestors.* New York: D. Appleton, 1911.

McSoley, Ray, with Larry Rothstein. *Dog Tales.* New York: Warner Books, 1988.

The Monks of New Skete. *How to Be Your Dog's Best Friend.* Boston: Little, Brown, 1978.

Reader's Digest Illustrated Book of Dogs, rev. ed. Pleasantville, N.Y.: Reader's Digest Association, Inc., 1989.

Ritvo, Harriet. *The Animal Estate.* Cambridge, Mass.: Harvard University Press, 1987.

Tortora, Daniel F. *The Right Dog for You.* New York: Simon & Schuster, 1983.

Woodhouse, Barbara. *No Bad Dogs.* New York: Summit, 1982.

Index